Kiss &
Sell

An AVA Book
Published by AVA Publishing SA
Chemin de la Joliette 2
Case postal 96
1000 Lausanne 6
Switzerland
Tel: +41 786 005 109
Email: enquiries@avabooks.ch

Distributed by Thames and Hudson (ex-North America)
181a High Holborn
London WC1V 7QX
United Kingdom
Tel: +44 20 7845 5000
Fax: +44 20 7845 5055
Email: sales@thameshudson.co.uk
www.thamesandhudson.com

Distributed by Sterling Publishing Co., Inc.
in the USA
387 Park Avenue South
New York, NY 10016-8810
Tel: +1 212 532 7160
Fax: +1 212 213 2495
www.sterlingpub.com

in Canada
Sterling Publishing
c/o Canadian Manda Group
One Atlantic Avenue, Suite 105
Toronto, Ontario M6K 3E7

English Language Support Office
AVA Publishing (UK) Ltd.
Tel: +44 1903 204 455
Email: enquiries@avabooks.co.uk

ISBN 2-88479-033-0

10 9 8 7 6 5 4 3 2 1

Original design concept by Bark Design
Layout by Refresh Design

Production and separations by
AVA Book Production Pte. Ltd., Singapore
Tel: +65 6334 8173
Fax: +65 6334 0752
Email: production@avabooks.com.sg

Kiss &
Sell

writing for
advertising

Robert Sawyer

ava | Academia
the environment of learning

contents

preface

I've had in the past the opportunity to watch Writer/Creative Directors review the portfolios of aspiring writers (including my own work). It is amusing at first, but within minutes grows tedious. The whole exercise is also more than a bit disingenuous. The reviewers are serious people and I believe it is their intent to offer good, honest advice. But in the end, the only help offered is insight into their own tastes. If they liked a headline, they smiled and complimented the writer. If it didn't amuse them, they confessed their lack of interest, and suggested ways to revise the work so it better conformed to their liking. In all these interviews, I've never once heard the reviewers ask, 'Did this ad work?' Nor did anyone inquire, 'What's here that compels the reader to choose your client's product?'

I think it's fair to say most ads fail. Whether this is true or not is beside the point because most clients think it to be true. What's more, few writers or art directors I've worked with believe in their work – except as examples of their creative gifts. Efficacy is seldom an issue, and then only when an account is in review. So what is the dynamic behind copy that does succeed? I believe successful copy is the result of two influences. The first is the tenacity of a campaign. The second, unfortunately, is entirely beyond the control of the writer, namely the Rightness of the product. By Rightness of the product, I mean qualities perceived as beneficial to a particular individual, in a particular place, at a particular moment.

Writers have very limited opportunity to create these places and moments, but they can capitalise on them. Which is to say, they can express this quality of Rightness. But to do it they must first want to know the product; want to understand their prospect's body/mind/heart; and want to learn the nature of the media employed to make the connection. Clever ideas and words, mastery of volume and intensity, are never enough. In practical terms, your work has little chance of succeeding unless it catches and pleases the eye, engages and persuades the mind, and finally, motivates and guides the hand.

Marshall McLuhan in *Understanding Media: The Extensions of Man* wrote, 'The ads are by far the best part of any magazine or newspaper. More pains and thought, more wit and art, go into making of an ad than into any prose feature of press or magazine.'

I think McLuhan got it half right. Good ads, ads that sell, are much smarter, more entertaining, and infinitely more honest than anything else a reader will find in his or her newspaper, magazine, or on television or a computer monitor. What ultimately makes copy work is its ability to make the connection between consumer and product inevitable. In this way the best copy achieves no less than the most seductive love letter. It persuades your beloved to love you, and for the foreseeable future, to love only you.

Robert Sawyer NYC 2004

foreword **steve hayden**

My creative philosophy, such as it is
First, let's get one thing clear. 99% of everything created by human beings sucks. Which means less than 1% of anything – including ads and reflections on creativity – is going to be excellent. I have rather high standards. So I've never been terribly happy with anything, including the work I'm best known for creating. In the sense that I'm unhappy at least 99% of the time, one might think that I am neither a very good creative director nor a well-balanced human being.

I do, however, believe that the 1% is worth all the pain.

That which is excellent changes everything. It's the basis of all human progress and whatever joy there may be in this troubled world. So excellence is worth pursuing despite the long odds.

More of my personal math
10% of everything is good, 60% of everything is just average, 20% of everything is bad, 9% is painfully awful, and about 1% is purely evil.

Now I believe these statistics apply to human beings as well. The object of management is to help average people do better than average and to give excellent people maximum opportunity to achieve excellence.

Apropos of genius, which may be rarer than excellence. Geniuses should simply be left alone to do whatever they're going to do. Assuming we can keep them in the neighbourhood, because they don't always stick around for very long.

David Ogilvy said we should hire gentlemen with brains. Of course, that was when you had ten employees for every million dollars in billing. These days, thanks to the agglomerations that have taken most of the profit out of our business, we can afford less than a quarter of a person for every million in dollars. So I suggested we change our policy to hiring assholes with talent. They're harder to live with, but they do deliver a better ROI than gentlemen and gentlewomen.

Avoiding the tar pit
It is every writer's duty to prevent the extinction of his or her clients. But sometimes the wooly mammoth will insist on going into the tar pit. It's warm and seems safe because very few predators will follow. Your instinct will be to do everything possible to save them, but sometimes, you just gotta let 'em go, hoping for rescue at a later time, once it dawns on them what they've done.

I've learned never to give up on a client. Once, when I was running the LA office of another agency, I insisted that we fire Coldwell Banker, one of the nation's leading real estate firms. It's a great company, but the woman running the advertising at the time was abusive, horrible and evil. So I insisted we dump them. The day we fired them, we were so happy we had an agency meeting and burned a Coldwell Banker sign in our lobby. Of course, the evil woman left a few months later, and Coldwell Banker went on to great financial and creative success with Grey.

The only excuse for resigning a client is if they insist on dragging you along with them into the tar pit. For example, Burger King. They had a hugely successful campaign in the early '80s centred on 'Have it your way'. Great jingle, great food spots. It was the most successful counter-positioning against McDonald's any fast food chain ever had. The agency fought long and hard to keep it, and the relationship frayed and then severed over the conflict. Burger King went into two decades of agency reviews and failed strategies, until they finally cycled back to a variation of 'Have it your way'. Had the agency simply gone along with the client, it would have constituted advertising malpractice and ruined their reputation with their other clients, most of whom were also challenger brands.

As a general rule, you have to take the long view of the relationship. You will have bad creative and account teams on your side from time to time, and it's your responsibility to be self-aware and tough enough to change staffing when it's not working. Once in a while, with enough trust and success, you can help clients correct their own staffing mistakes. But in most cases, you have to wait until they discover their own errors. Ultimately you have to play the cards you're dealt. Incompetence on the part of the client is no excuse for non-performance on your part. You must do everything you can to get them out of the tar pit to the top of the grassy hill where they can prosper and multiply.

Advertising is, quite literally, air pollution. We're soaking in it all the time. So breakthrough is certainly the first order of business. I have actually heard clients ask for ads that are not 'too breakthrough', because their first order of business is to not get in trouble. They want to do a responsible programme, spend a certain amount of money which falls within established parameters for their business and industry, report success at the end of the year, and get on with their lives.

The real objective of these clients is to preserve their employment.

However, the best brands, as a rule, tend to have the top leadership of the company directly involved in the process of making advertising. If you can find yourself a Steve Jobs or Paul Presler or Tom Ford or Phil Knight or Fred Smith, your career is assured. Because even when these companies build elaborate structures, as size and success will force them to do, they maintain an entrepreneurial spirit that demands excellence at all times.

And if we, poor humans that we are, can move from < 1% to > 1% in all we do, our careers are made and fame resounds.

Steve Hayden NYC 2004

A native of California, Steve Hayden began his career in Detroit, writing for General Motors. Returning to California, Hayden divided his time between advertising and TV scriptwriting before choosing advertising. He honed his craft on Toyota at the Clinton E. Frank agency, then on Mazda at Foote Cone & Belding, until Jay Chiat spotted one of his ads and hired him. Hayden opened Chiat Day's office in New York in 1980, and in San Francisco in 1981. With Lee Chow, he made ad history creating the famous '1984' TV spot for Apple. In 1986, Hayden was named Chairman/CEO of BBDO's West Coast operations. There, he helped Apple win the highest market share in its history, while trebling the size of his agency by winning assignments from Pioneer Electronics, Northrop-Grumman, Pizza Hut, and Dodge, among others. In 1994, Ogilvy invited Steve to assume the newly created role of 'Brand Steward' for IBM. In 2001, he was promoted to Vice Chairman of the worldwide agency, to act as Shelly Lazarus' creative partner to global brands.

foreword **bob greenberg**
on writing for the interactive channel

The first thing that most of us forget is that the interactive channel is only nine years old. We're just beginning to figure out what works online, especially regarding writing for the Web. Now we're asking ourselves how will copywriting change when crafting messages that appear on interactive and wireless devices? The truth is, we're forced to invent as we go. Think of what the move from LPs to CDs did to liner notes. Other communication channels have matured. Print, radio and television (and for that matter, popular music and film) have their own set of rules. It's well known what you can do with a page of copy, a billboard, a radio spot or a 30-second TV commercial.

Traditional media is where most writers work or started their careers. When you transition into the interactive channel, the mistake most often made is trying to repurpose what you have been doing offline for the Web. This doesn't work. Each channel has a different structure and different demands. And online there are varying demands depending on the project. A banner doesn't read like a website. What's more, there's the audience to consider. The Web is about the audience. You can't address an IT professional visiting the IBM site in the same way as you talk to a kid from Harlem going to Nikebasketball.com. The behavior of online users, specifically how they consume information from a site is different from their approach to reading a magazine or viewing a television spot. Whether they're young millennials, or older literary types, they scan. People go to the Web to find what interests them and then they use that information in the way that best meets their needs. So it's the audience that matters, and it's important, as writers, that you share its tastes and desires. Our writers on Purina love animals. Our writers for Nike Basketball live and breathe hoops. Writing for the Web is more like writing for a niche magazine than creating an ad. Ultimately you will be providing information about a product, service and a brand.

TV spots in the future will be made to build awareness. Their purpose will be to drive you to the Web. It's already begun. Today, there's almost no information conveyed in commercials, the ads are short experiences that end in a URL. For instance, to fully experience Nike's message, you have to go online. Ultimately, car spots are designed to drive consumers to their sites. The other important thing to understand is that the central idea in any linear medium is story telling. There's always a beginning, middle and an end. Techniques and innovations evolve, but basically TV spots, music videos, radio spots or feature films share this language. But the interactive channel is bi-directional, experiential and non-linear. For instance, on the Web there's no one path, rather multiple avenues and access points. As a result vast quantities of information can be included on a website. The IBM site has over six million pages. This begs the question, just because you can include everything, should you? So we have an interesting job ahead, of not only creating content but also devising the rules and guidelines that will shape it.

The Web is transitioning. We've moved from brochureware, which was essentially an online catalogue, to e-commerce, which was basically transactional, to the intelligent, experiential Web. So how do you write for a medium that is anything but static? Look at a lot of websites. Check out the award sites. Study the medium. It is a good idea to acquire some expertise, to learn enough about something to be able to write an article or even a book. If you're lucky enough to be passionate about something, become an expert in it. Soon there will be courses at universities that teach writing for the Web. But for now, we have created guidelines that work for our clients and trained our writers because there have been no courses that taught this craft.

We look for people who are inquisitive, who have ideas and are able to think metaphorically. We also look for people who have specific interests or expertise. But most importantly, we find people who know and love this medium. Also, know as much as you can about everything you can. Be on top of what's good. And this is really important. Interactive media is not going to displace traditional media, but it is still important to know how to write across multiple channels, because nothing is going away. The interactive channel will continue to grow in significance, so being able to effectively write for the channel, whether it is a banner, website, email or for a wireless device is a valuable skill to cultivate.

So what's my advice? Adapt. Keep learning. Stay out there. You can always find time to unplug, but you're either with the flow or you're not. You already have the tools, but if you want to be good, you have to work hard – really hard. And finally, if you have something to say, don't be afraid to say it. Since the rules are just being made, there is a tremendous opportunity to make your mark and have a hand in crafting the future.

Robert M. Greenberg
Chairman and CEO R/GA

Since 1977 Greenberg has led the vision for R/GA, a 250-person strategic interactive agency based in the digital medium. He is committed to developing a new business model based on the convergence of narrowband, broadband and wireless technologies, while continuing to embrace the importance of creative excellence and innovative technology solutions. The company develops digital projects and delivers innovative solutions to Fortune 500 companies, combining non-linear executions of entertainment, communications and marketing under one roof.

Greenberg was the first to bring together the disparate areas of print, television commercials and feature films into one company and RGA's body of work spans 400 feature films and 4,000 television commercials. Along the way he has won almost every industry award for creativity including the Academy Award, Clios and Cannes Lions. Among his most notable awards are the Cooper-Hewitt National Design Award and the Chrysler Award for Innovation in Design that was accompanied by a show of R/GA's work at the San Francisco MOMA. He has been named as the 2004 Cyber Lions Jury President.

He serves on the boards of numerous schools and organisations focused on the importance of design and the creative process including: President of the Art Directors Club Board of Directors; Brooklyn Academy of Music; Dean's Council Advisory Board of Tisch School of the Arts; Parsons School of Design and the Studio School of Art. Greenberg is currently an Adjunct Professor at New York University Tisch School of the Arts, ITP programme.

foreword **peter arnell**

An image speaks a thousand words

As someone who is not known for creating 'copy' in the traditional sense of the word, it struck me as particularly interesting to be asked to write a forward for a book on the art of copywriting. My message to everyone reading this is: Copy is more than words.

Copy is an idea that needs to be brought to life through a variety of visual and verbal techniques. Copy is a viewer's takeaway. Copy is a resulting feeling. Copy is what you still remember long after you have turned the page.

As I am a man of little words, I will keep this short and sweet.

Words explain but images speak.

Here is an ad for Donna Karan 'Bath and Body'. It was noted for its ability to convey brand image, product attributes, consumer benefits and user aspiration. It uses no words. The logo is there so the viewer knows what to buy.

If you can put into your own words what this ad says to you, then, in fact, you are being spoken to by the most compelling form of copy: the image that speaks a thousand words.

Peter Arnell NYC 2003

DONNA KARAN
NEW YORK
BATH & BODY

Creative Director: Peter Arnell Art Director: Peter Arnell Photographer: Peter Arnell
Courtesy of Donna Karan New York.

Peter Arnell is the Chairman and Chief Creative Officer of Arnell Group, a brand ideation and experience marketing company specializing in integrated branding, strategy and communications solutions. An architect and designer by training, at Columbia and Princeton Universities respectively, Mr. Arnell began his career writing and designing books on architecture and design. He has published over 18 books including academic monographs on Frank Gehry, Aldo Rossi and James Stirling. His success in publishing led to creating the identity for Donna Karan, as well as the groundbreaking DKNY brand.

Mr Arnell has played a significant role in establishing the brand platforms and marketing strategies for brands as varied as Consolidated Edison and the consumer electronics giant, Samsung Group. Mr. Arnell was also instrumental in redefining such brands as Polaroid, Skytel and Banana Republic. Other work includes, his revitalisation of Hanes Hosiery in 1997, through the brand's breakthrough association with Tina Turner. He further pioneered product placement as part of an integrated marketing solution by placing Ray-Ban sunglasses in the film, *Men in Black*. Mr Arnell has further integrated entertainment and marketing with campaigns such as the proprietary music programme partnership with Pepsi and Universal Music Group and the rewriting of the Chrysler brand language including Chrysler's unique partnership with Celine Dion.

Most recently, Mr Arnell has reinvigorated the Reebok brand, along with conceptualizing and launching the highly successful RBK brand for Reebok incorporating lifestyle with Hip-Hop artists, athletes and featuring a new apparel line by rapper Jay-Z. In addition, by imbedding musical talent Justin Timberlake and the Neptunes into McDonald's culture, Mr Arnell has caused a dramatic turn-around in the perception of the McDonald's brand.

introduction

Kiss & Sell: Writing for Advertising is organised so that it can be opened at any point and engage the reader in a discussion on the craft of copywriting. Various media and topics – from print and broadcast to naming and interactive media – are discussed, as well as the tactics and strategies employed by writers – from the use of heavy text to the complete absence of it. Insights and anecdotes from some of today's leading practitioners of the craft supplement the author's analysis and observations.

Kiss & Sell does not judge the work it uses to illustrate its various points. There are no right and wrong examples. The ads are not dissected. Instead, the book helps students as well as professionals to distinguish between their tastes or preferences and an objective or critical reading of the examples. On a thorough study of *Kiss & Sell*, readers will have a clear understanding of the various dynamics at work in effective copywriting. And they can sit down and write copy.

The chapter called 'Writing Copy' is the heart of the book and the most extensive. It is extensive because each idea, each approach, each technique, each type of advertising are separate sections, ranging from two to six pages. The brief text that begins each section is the synthesis of that section. And the captions, accompanying the examples of advertisements, dissect and analyse each example in a short, succinct manner.

Each section is self-contained. And, within the sections, each example of the advertisements with the accompanying captions is self-contained. It isn't absolutely necessary that you read the introductory text of a section. Feel free to go straight to the examples and their captions. You can always return to the text later.

Open the book at any page and read at random, if you wish. Or read progressively from the front to the back.

The advertisements are reproduced large enough so that you can read the text in them.

And these reproductions abound.
Read them.
Read them without a critical eye, if possible.
Read them whether you think they're clever or not.
Read them even if you're not interested in the product or company
Don't ask yourself, 'Are they good?', but rather, 'What did the copywriter intend and did he/she succeed?'.

Presumably they did succeed. That's why they are here. Which means that there is no negative criticism of them. And you will not read, for example, 'The copywriter should have done this or that and didn't.' The focus here is, as it might likewise be with you, on success.

how to get the **most** out of this book

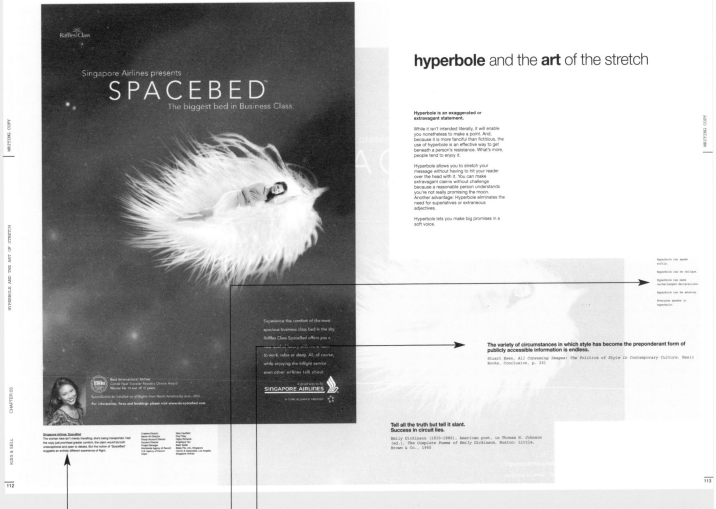

hyperbole and the art of the stretch

Hyperbole is an exaggerated or extravagant statement.

While it isn't intended literally, it will enable you nonetheless to make a point. And, because it is more fanciful than fictitious, the use of hyperbole is an effective way to get beneath a person's resistance. What's more, people tend to enjoy it.

Hyperbole allows you to stretch your message without having to hit your reader over the head with it. You can make extravagant claims without challenge because a reasonable person understands you're not really promising the moon. Another advantage: Hyperbole eliminates the need for superlatives or extraneous adjectives.

Hyperbole lets you make big promises in a soft voice.

The variety of circumstances in which style has become the preponderant form of publicly accessible information is endless.
Stuart Ewen, *All Consuming Images: The Politics of Style in Contemporary Culture.* Basic Books, Conclusion, p. 261

Tell all the truth but tell it slant. Success in circuit lies.
Emily Dickinson (1830–1886), American poet, in Thomas H. Johnson (ed.), *The Complete Poems of Emily Dickinson.* Boston: Little, Brown & Co., 1960

How to proceed

Begin at the beginning of the book and journey to the end.

Go to only the sections that interest you.

Look at the sections at random.

The captions of the advertisements explain:
1. How copywriters solved the problems.
2. What they were thinking – their points of view.
3. Why they made the choices they made.
4. What marketing strategies they developed.
5. Why a certain approach was used for a certain client, product, or service.
6. Why the copy is effective.
7. What techniques and devices were called on and why.

The quotations, placed here and there on the pages:
1. Reinforce the lesson of the section.
2. Offer insights into the theories of advertising pioneers or renowned professionals.
3. Provide inspiration through the musings of historical literary or philosophical giants.
4. Entertain and amuse.

The sidebars are:
1. Pithy examples.
2. Pertinent details.
3. Dos and don'ts.
4. Excerpts from the text and captions.
5. Word and term definitions.
6. Aphorisms

Real advertisements from the real world
Kiss & Tell is not an awards-show annual or a review of prize-winning advertisements. The examples here were largely selected at random, since this is how advertisements are seen in the real world. This approach was also taken because most copywriters rarely get to choose their clients or assignments.

The advertisements in the book are primarily from magazines. This choice was made because print advertising best illustrates everything that can be said and explained about writing copy. Another reason is that writing for TV and interactive media is primarily a collaborative effort, involving a number of professional specialties, each central to the success of the work, much like movies.

And, about the real world, if a copywriter is only able to produce good work for 'fancy', high-profile clients, his career will probably be thwarted. Most copywriters never work for these clients. This is the reason that few award-winning advertisements have been included in this book. What's here are real advertisements from the real world.

chapter **01**

what is
copywriting?

[Copywriting is] about making real how the products or services we write about bring improvement, comfort and even a bit of magic to a single human life.

Ed McCabe in *The Copywriter's Bible: How 32 of the World's Best Advertising Writers Write their Copy*, Hove, UK: RotoVision, 2000, p. 121

ABSOLUT ORIGIN.

ALL ABSOLUT COMES FROM A SINGLE SOURCE. The same aquifer. The same fields of winter wheat. The same distillery in Åhus, Sweden. ALL ABSOLUT is ABSOLUT.

OUR DEVOTION TO PERFECTION IS ABSOLUT.

Absolut: Absolut Origin
In this new campaign, Absolut has shifted its focus. After years of punning headlines that paired the Absolut name with cool or contemporary artists and designers, as well as places and concepts, the new copy looks inward to the product itself. Here, the Absolut name is joined with the word 'origin'. Origin is a metaphor for 'purity'. Is purity an issue for consumers of vodka? The brand makes it one.

Creative Director	Joseph Mazzaferro
Art Director	Andy Hall
Agency	TBWA/Chiat/Day New York
Client	Absolut

There is one unalterable fact that differentiates copywriting from all other forms of writing. An ad is never an end in itself. It always refers to something beyond it, the product.

Tony Cox, producer of notable radio and TV spots, in *The Copywriter's Bible: How 32 of the World's Best Advertising Writers Write their Copy*, Hove, UK: RotoVision, 2000, p. 30

ideas first. **words** follow

Copywriters write. Or do they?

Copywriters are storytellers.

Their job is to tell the right story to the right audience at the right volume.

Some writers think of themselves as image builders. Others try not to write advertisements.

But everyone with experience and expertise agrees: writing copy is different from all other forms of writing. And the advertisement itself is not an end in itself.

Ultimately, copywriting specifically and an advertisement generally are about the product or the service.

This is why a book about copywriting – this book about copywriting – is not so as much about words as it is about ideas and how ideas can be shaped to make a sale. Writers indifferent to the sale will not be happy in the advertising business.

Advertising is about the product or the service, not about the advertising.

Selling something to someone is ultimately all there is.

Copywriting is a form unique unto itself.

Copywriters select positive truths and omit negative ones.

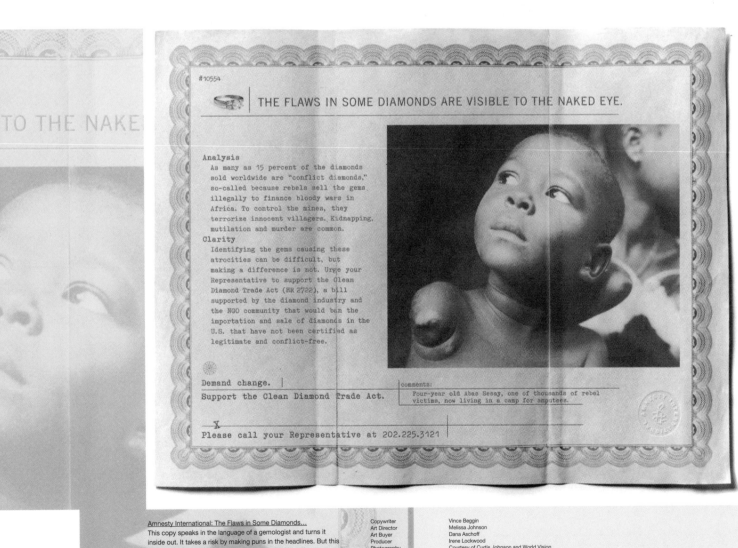

#10554

THE FLAWS IN SOME DIAMONDS ARE VISIBLE TO THE NAKED EYE.

Analysis
As many as 15 percent of the diamonds sold worldwide are "conflict diamonds," so-called because rebels sell the gems illegally to finance bloody wars in Africa. To control the mines, they terrorize innocent villagers. Kidnapping, mutilation and murder are common.

Clarity
Identifying the gems causing these atrocities can be difficult, but making a difference is not. Urge your Representative to support the Clean Diamond Trade Act (HR 2722), a bill supported by the diamond industry and the NGO community that would ban the importation and sale of diamonds in the U.S. that have not been certified as legitimate and conflict-free.

Demand change.
Support the Clean Diamond Trade Act.

comments:
Four-year old Abas Sesay, one of thousands of rebel victims, now living in a camp for amputees.

X
Please call your Representative at 202.225.3121

Amnesty International: The Flaws in Some Diamonds...
This copy speaks in the language of a gemologist and turns it inside out. It takes a risk by making puns in the headlines. But this play on words wasn't intended to elicit a smile, but rather to open the reader's eyes. It also demonstrates how to communicate outrage without shouting.

Copywriter — Vince Beggin
Art Director — Melissa Johnson
Art Buyer — Dana Aschoff
Producer — Irene Lockwood
Photography — Courtesy of Curtis Johnson and World Vision
Agency — Martin Williams
Client — Amnesty International (Adotei Akwei, Helen Garrett)

IDEAS FIRST. WORDS FOLLOW

Style. Unlike any other.

Style.

Every Mercedes-Benz is designed to the most exacting specifications, then crafted with attention to the last 1/16 of an in[

Mercedes-Benz: 'Tailor'
Style. Unlike Any Other
What might have been a single, cohesive phrase – 'Style Unlike Any
Other' – is here broken into two fragments. 'Style', perhaps the most
overused word in automobile advertising, is used alone. 'Unlike Any
Other' follows. The use of a period after each is important. The form
may be grammatically incorrect, but it nevertheless powerfully
emphasises 'Style', imbuing it with a surprising resonance
(see also pages 58 and 118).

Copywriter	Ben Hieger
Co-Creative Directors/Partners	Andy Hirsch, Randy Saitta
Art Director	Craig Cimmino
Photographer	Darran Rees
Agency	Merkley + Partners New York
Client	Mercedes-Benz

Courtesy of Mercedes-Benz USA

Fully expect your expectations to be raised. Call 1-800-FOR-MERCEDES. Or visit MBUSA.com.

Mercedes-Benz

A copywriter, like a lawyer, builds cases for clients by selecting truths that are positive and omitting truths that aren't.

Paul Silverman, in *The Copywriter's Bible: How 32 of the World's Best Advertising Writers Write their Copy*, Hove, UK: RotoVision, 2000, p. 150

It's not easy to avoid sounding like an advertisement. I can spend hours on a single sentence, and I have sometimes done 20 drafts of a long ad.

Indra Sinha, in *The Copywriter's Bible: How 32 of the World's Best Advertising Writers Write their Copy*, Hove, UK: RotoVision, 2000

What is it that copywriters actually write? The answer to this question isn't obvious in a business where words appear to be have become optional.

In some advertisements, the logo is enough to make the sale. In others, the right music might do it. So the sooner a copywriter learns to treat copy as only one element of the whole advertisement, the better. The copy is part of the sometimes dominant, sometimes recessive elements in the soup of signs and symbols that compose a communication.

While writing copy requires creativity, good copy is a craft a writer learns, with much practice, over time. There's no doubt that flashes of poetic inspiration do occur. From 'Melts in your mouth, not in your hand' and 'Think small', to 'Just do it' and 'Let's motor', lines of copy have appeared that seemed divinely inspired. But ultimately one learns that it's sheer doggedness that gets the job done. It is an article of faith that good copy is the result of writing and rewriting and rewriting again.

But how do you write good copy? First, you must have a faith in words, know that words have power, that words can move people to action.

But what are the secrets to writing good copy? Are there any? The often chanted mantra of the professionals is, 'Edit, edit, edit'. Others simply murmur, 'Simplify'. Many copy supervisors and creative directors in advertising agencies often invoke American novelist Mark Twain's admonition, 'Kill all your darlings'. He meant, 'Stop holding on to those sentences, those words, those phrases that you hold precious and dear but don't work – except in your mind.'

In the end, it's not your work:
It's important to keep in mind that many of the dynamics behind the success or failure of your work are often beyond your control. Schedules, budgets, bad research, a bored boss, a jealous colleague, inappropriate media buys, illogical, or as likely, irrational client interference, intra- and inter-office politics, even the opinion of the client's spouse, these and a hundred variables will determine the final shape of your work. So while you must always take your work seriously, you must never take its outcome personally.

Advertising is an environmental striptease for a world of abundance.

Marshall McLuhan, Introduction to Wilson Bryan Key, *Subliminal Seduction: Ad Media's Manipulation of a Not So Innocent America*, New York: Signet Books, 1974, p. vii

Copy is only one element in a communication's signs and symbols.

The headline in the pantheon of icons won't pop into your head every day.

Good, simple copy results from writing, rewriting, and rewriting.

Writing good copy is a learnable craft.

not exactly **prose**. not exactly **poetry**

deeper

Consulting Services
Delivered on-site, outsourced or on-demand.

IBM: Deeper
When an industry giant chooses a single word to introduce its new
consulting division, then the expectation is that one word will speak
volumes. 'Deeper' has a double meaning here: that IBM has
considerable depth of available resources and that a client who
engages IBM will experience an appreciable degree of relief.

Creative Directors	Andy Berndt, John McNeil
Copywriter	Larry Goldstein
Art Director	Andy Gray
Photographer	J.P. Fruchet/Getty Images
Agency	Ogilvy & Mather New York
Client	IBM

NOT EXACTLY PROSE. NOT EXACTLY POETRY

Strange things happen in 10 feet of visibility.

Twenty-five years at the helm. Over 60,000 hours logged. Thousands of tons of cargo hauled. And there's still nothing you can do when fog rolls in. On top of the damage to the vessel, your fuel tank empties into the surrounding river. Now you're without a ship and responsible for thousands of dollars in cleanup costs.

WQIS marine pollution insurance anticipates what you can't.

Things go wrong, from bad luck to terrible accidents. Which is why more vessel owners and operators choose WQIS for their marine pollution insurance. It's a fact, no one has more experience cleaning up spills, or offers more innovative coverage to the marine community.

Sail with Experience

Have your broker contact WQIS for a quote today.
212-292-8700
www.wqis.com

WQIS

I'm not really an ad man. I'm just a guy who likes to write about cool things.

Ken Segall, partner and worldwide creative director on Intel account, Euro RSCG Worldwide, told to Robert Sawyer

CHAPTER 01

KISS & SELL

If advertising is not an official or state *art*, it is nonetheless clearly *art*.

Michael Schudson, *Advertising, The Uneasy Persuasion: Its Dubious Impact on American Society*, New York: Basic Books, 1984, p. 222

"That's it?"

beside him in the bottom bunk, lying there until he fell asleep, assuring him that Dick was merely hiding at a friend's house, that he would be found and brought home.

"But whose house would he hide in?" Cole pointed out. "What friend?"

Christmas came tainted. When Cole was asked what he wanted, he said that he wanted to go home and meant L.A. He wished for nothing else. Lizzie flew in from California, once more without her grandmother. This time, the woman had turned tail when she saw the cab at the curb of the nursing home.

"If you want to see her," Lizzie told her mother nonchalantly as she reached to switch on the car radio, "you're going to have to get your ass back to L.A."

Christmas Eve, Ann woke from a dream that it was Dick she'd found dead, swirling there in the swimming pool.

"What's wrong?" Richard asked, half asleep, his kind blind hand reaching, out of habit, to reassure her.

"Nothing," she said, sliding away from his touch.

Cole's twelfth birthday fell on a bitter January Saturday. Under duress, he'd invited three boys, somewhat randomly—they were in his grade, they lived nearby. The doorbell rang at noon, although the party wouldn't start until four; the cake was still baking, the decorations unhung. Ann opened the door to find Dick's parents on her doorstep, holding a puppy with a bow around its neck.

"We couldn't just sit there doing nothing," Nancy explained as Ann invited them inside. Her husband came in reluctantly, never having entered Ann's home before. But both the weather and the situation were too raw now for him to stand outside. The couple looked haunted, as if drained of a shared vital fluid. It occurred to Ann that they couldn't be completely sane at this moment. "We're looking for Dick," Nancy said. "We thought he might have come to Colorado. Gary saw it in a dream, the KOA campground in Fort Collins."

Dick's father blushed deeply inside the hood of his hunter's camouflage jacket. He was not a man accustomed to sharing his dreams, to having them made public. Nancy touched his sleeve with her free hand. This was how they stayed together, Ann saw—by giving permission, comfort, by being so much the other's missing half.

"Sit down," she said, indicating the couch before the hearth, where she'd just lit a fire. "Richard and Cole are out buying hot dogs. It's Cole's birthday." The smell of the cake baking was in the air; balloons were drifting under the dining-room table.

"And we brought him a present," Nancy said. "There's nothing like a Rot-

a **craft.** not an **art**

Good copy doesn't have to be original. It doesn't have to have literary value. And a good copywriter doesn't have to be highly knowledgeable about proper grammar and syntax.

What good copywriters must be is persuasive. Good copy is a good argument, and well-argued cases are seldom blurted out. They are built in a logical almost mechanical sequence. Word by word, sentence by sentence, a copywriter builds his client's case. And good copywriting benefits from scrupulous attention paid to detail.

Copywriters succeed when they write a word, a phrase, or a sentence that prompts readers to want to hear what's next and next and next. It can become easy when writing to a particular person. When you know the people you're addressing, then you know in advance what they want to take away. They want to know that a particular car is faster, a certain company is more innovative, one toy is more fun.

It's possible to touch readers every time you try. But it rarely happens. To hone the craft, you must rewrite and rewrite until the words tell the truth.

How to arrive at the truth:
1. Write the story.
2. Read it out loud to yourself.
3. Find something objectionable in it.
4. Answer the objection.
5. Refute your own answer.
6. Start over.
7. Find something objectionable again.
8. Defend your argument.
9. Repeat until you persuade yourself that your argument is true.

Learning the craft
Ian Reichenthal, who wrote for creative shops including Cliff Freeman and Wieden + Kennedy, tells this story: 'As a junior, I had an opportunity to watch a number of senior writers at work. They were all good, but one stood out. After a couple of weeks I asked him if he could teach me to be a better writer. This man told me, "Don't worry about getting better. Just get faster."'

The quality this writer possessed wasn't simply the ability to turn out one ad after another, but to look at his work with a cold eye. Over time this writer learned to throw out what was rubbish sooner, and focus only on the most promising concepts. He wrote faster, and the faster he wrote, the less attached he was to every clever pun or brilliant line. In the end he achieved the naturalness of a runner who avoids potholes without seeing them, or a card sharp who discards a hand without a glance.

If you're not coming in on Saturday, don't bother coming in on Sunday either.

A long-running joke at the Chiat Day advertising agency.

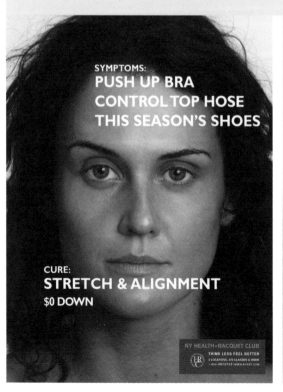

SYMPTOMS:
PUSH UP BRA
CONTROL TOP HOSE
THIS SEASON'S SHOES

CURE:
STRETCH & ALIGNMENT
$0 DOWN

NY HEALTH+RACQUET CLUB
THINK LESS·FEEL BETTER

SYMPTOMS:
STUDIO APARTMENT
CROWDED SUBWAY
CRAMPED CUBICLE

CURE:
HATHA YOGA
$0 DOWN

NY HEALTH+RACQUET CLUB
THINK LESS·FEEL BETTER

SYMPTOMS:
LINE AT THE BANK
LINE AT THE DELI
LINE TO GET IN LINE

CURE:
FOUR MIDTOW
LOCATIONS

NEW YORK

Everything considered, work is less boring than amusing oneself.

Charles Baudelaire (1821–1867), French poet, *Mon coeur mis à nu: journal intime* (1864), Geneva: Claude Pichois, 2001

SYMPTOMS:
NEW JOB
NEW GIRLFRIEND
NEW DOG

CURE:
SUNRISE MEDITATION
$0 DOWN

NY HEALTH+RACQUET CLUB

THINK LESS FEEL BETTER
8 LOCATIONS. 570 CLASSES A WEEK
1-800-HRCBEST/WWW.NYHRC.COM

New York Health + Racquet Club: Symptoms: Cure campaign
Is a story good because it rings true? Or does it ring true because it's a good story? The stories here call on two-word scenarios: 'symptoms' and 'cure'. They're sufficient to state the essence of the problem and the succinct solution. Anything more is unnecessary. Though the client is local and the potential customer a young urbanite, the approach is universal.

Creative Director	Steve Conner
Copywriter	Steve Conner
Art Director	Diana Wilson
Photographer	Steve Conner
Agency	The STEVE Agency
Client	New York Health + Racquet Club (NYHRC)

All ads conceived, created and executed by The STEVE Agency.

23

IF WE'VE LEARNED ONE THING IN 30 YEARS OF BUILDING RANGE ROVERS, IT IS THIS:
AN OSTRICH EGG WILL FEED EIGHT MEN.

Range Rover: An Ostrich Egg Will Feed Eight Men

Adults, like children, love stories. This ad combines devices from both oral and literary storytelling traditions. It starts with a raconteur's irresistable set-up and proceeds in the manner of both a tale told at a bar and in adventure-travel literature.

Group Creative Directors	David Crawford, Jeremy Postaer
Copywriters	Michael Buss, Jeremy Postaer
Art Directors	Rob Story, David Crawford
Agency	GSD&M
Client	Land Rover

The list of sins committed by advertising is limited only by the creativity of its critics.

Jerry Kirkpatrick, 'A Philosophic Defense of Advertising',
Journal of Advertising, 1986, vol. 15, no 2

Words should be weighed, not counted.

Yiddish proverb in Robert I. Fitzhenry (ed.), *The Harper Book of Quotations*, New York HarperPerennnial, 1993 (3rd ed.)

I suspect that there is no other single profession that does more to contribute to our annoying linguistic convolutions than advertising, unless it's politics.

Jef Richards, advertising professor, The University of Texas at Austin, 1997

Learn what persuades.

If you know who your readers are, you'll know what they want to know.

Good copy is a good argument.

Copywriters don't have to be more literate than their audience.

I AM A SHELL.

I CAN FIGHT CANCER. I AM *MERCENARIA MERCENARIA*.
I HAVE AN EXTRACT IN MY SHELL THAT HAS THE POWER TO
SLOW CANCERS IN MICE. I HAVE THE POWER TO BE THE NEXT
PENICILLIN. I AM MORE THAN A SHELL.

I AM A NETWORK.

I CAN TURN SHELLS INTO MEDICINE. I HAVE THE POWER TO
MOVE CLINICAL TRIALS ONLINE SO NEW DRUGS GET TO
MARKET FASTER. I HAVE THE POWER TO PROTECT A PATIENT'S
PRIVACY. I CAN USE THE POWER OF E-LEARNING TO LET
DOCTORS SHARE RESEARCH WITH OTHER DOCTORS. I THINK
SHARING IS CARING. I AM MORE THAN A NETWORK.

CISCO SYSTEMS

THIS IS THE POWER OF THE NETWORK. now.
cisco.com/powernow

Cisco Systems: I Am a Shell. I Am a Network
Here is a simple story told simply about something that's not simple.
The advertisement didn't set out to change readers' minds, but rather to
reinforce what readers already suspect. And the truth offered here is
that Cisco Systems is the partner you can trust, because, in this case,
this company knows the true power of a network.

Creative Directors	Dan Burrier, Gavin Milner
Copywriter	Steve P. Williams
Art Director	Justin Hooper
Photographer	Christian Stohl
Producer	Leslie D'Acri
Agency	Ogilvy & Mather
Client	Cisco Systems

You must know what you're talking about. In order to be informative – never mind persuasive – you need to know how the car is put together, how the chicken is taken apart, what the surfactant does, what to expect in the foreign country, in what way is the oil refinery 'refined', etc.

Bob Levenson, advertising executive and author, in *The Copywriter's Bible: How 32 of the World's Best Advertising Writers Write their Copy*, Hove, UK: RotoVision, 2000

Curiosity about life in all of its aspects, I think, is still the secret of great creative people.

Leo Burnett, in *100 LEO's*, Chicago, IL: Leo Burnett Company, p. 26

You can observe a lot just by watching.

Yogi Berra, New York Yankee, Baseball Hall of Fame Catcher, celebrated for his original use of language

Read everything in sight, even graffiti.

Know everything about everything before you begin.

Keep a folder of ideas, even if some seem stupid at the moment.

Resist generalities.

Alaris: One Less Thing to Worry About
If you know one undeniable fact, state it. If there's a single issue that captures the entire proposition, call it out. If there's one significant promise to be made, make it. The copy need not be fancy; Alaris's copy isn't. But it should ring true to the reader.

Creative Director/Art Director	Dean Alexander, Robert Sawyer
Creative Director/Copywriter	Robert Sawyer
Design Production	Paul Rodriguez
Design Firm	Alexander Design Associates Inc.
Account Directors	Peter Nolan, Dana Weissfield, Audrey Ronis-Tobin
Brand Marketing Specialist	Trudi Bresner
Agency	T. Bresner Associates
Client	Alaris Medical

The truth isn't the truth until people believe you, and they can't believe you if they don't know what you're saying, and they can't know what you're saying if they don't listen to you, and they won't listen to you if you're not interesting, and you won't be interesting unless you say things imaginatively, originally, freshly.

William 'Bill' Bernbach, advertising pioneer, *Bill Bernbach Said…*, New York: DDB Needham Worldwide, 1989

It is good to know the truth, but it is better to speak of palm trees.

Arabic proverb in Robert I. Fitzhenry (ed.), *The Harper Book of Quotations*, New York: Harper Perennial, 1993 (3rd ed.)

it's **what** you know

Good copywriters read. They read everything they can get their eyes on. They read newspapers and magazines, novels and histories. They read catalogues, annual reports, advertising awards-show books. They interrupt a walk down a street to read a snipe or graffiti. Some read the advertising classics – from Rosser Reeves's to David Ogilvy's. So, read about advertising, public relations, and persuasive writing – not just this book.

Some copywriters also collect facts and gossip. Advertising pioneer Leo Burnett kept a folder called 'Corny Language' in the lower drawer of his desk. In it he recorded idioms and 'aptly expressed' ideas. Another folder he titled 'Ads Worth Keeping' he added to over 25 years. The advertising impresario, Peter Arnell, continues to fill dozens of notebooks with clippings, quotes, drawings and notes.

Some copywriters don't just write for advertising; they write prose, poetry, or screenplays. But for most copywriters, the advertisement's the thing. To them advertising copy can be a piece of writing as legitimate and satisfying as a movie-script credit or a poem in *The New Yorker* or *Puck*.

THE LEXUS I·S

Daytona. Watkins Glen. Road America. These are the daily commutes of the Team Lexus I·S. Where it takes on the likes of BMW, Porsche and Audi, and does exceedingly well, thank you very much. Now granted, the rigors of your daily driving may not be as demanding as those of the professional race circuit. In fact, we know they're not. But isn't it nice to know you can explode off the line with a 3.0-liter, 215-horsepower in-line 6, should the need arise? Or carve decisively into a curve with confidence and discernible adrenaline flow, knowing the power-assisted rack-and-pinion steering and sport-tuned suspension are at your command? If you're not sure of the answer, ask a Team Lexus driver. And get ready for an earful.

IF IT **HANDLES** LIKE A **PERFORMANCE CAR,** THAT'S BECAUSE IT IS.

Can an automobile delight, comfort, fascinate and energize you? Take lexus.com for a test drive. The Passionate Pursuit of Perfection.

 **LEXUS**

Insisting that he never writes anything until he knows everything there is to know: *When I write, it's with explosive passion and bravado. With a tinge of insanity even. But before I write, I'm painstaking, plodding, disciplined.*

Ed McCabe, founder, Scali, McCabe, Sloves advertising agency, New York City, in *The Copywriter's Bible: How 32 of the World's Best Advertising Writers Write their Copy*, Hove, UK: RotoVision, 2000, p. 120

Lexus: If It Handles Like a Performance Car...
If you want to alter a perception, know where you're going. Avoid generalities. Take risks. Name names. Know the players. State the facts. Stay on track. That's what the writer did here.

Copywriter	Jon Pearce
Art Director	Jim Dearing
Chief Creative	Tom Cordner
Photographer	David LeBon
Traffic	Wendi Green
Studio Artist	Tracy Thomas
Print Producer	Dana Ruiz
Account Executive	Rudi Anthony
Agency	Team One
Client	Lexus

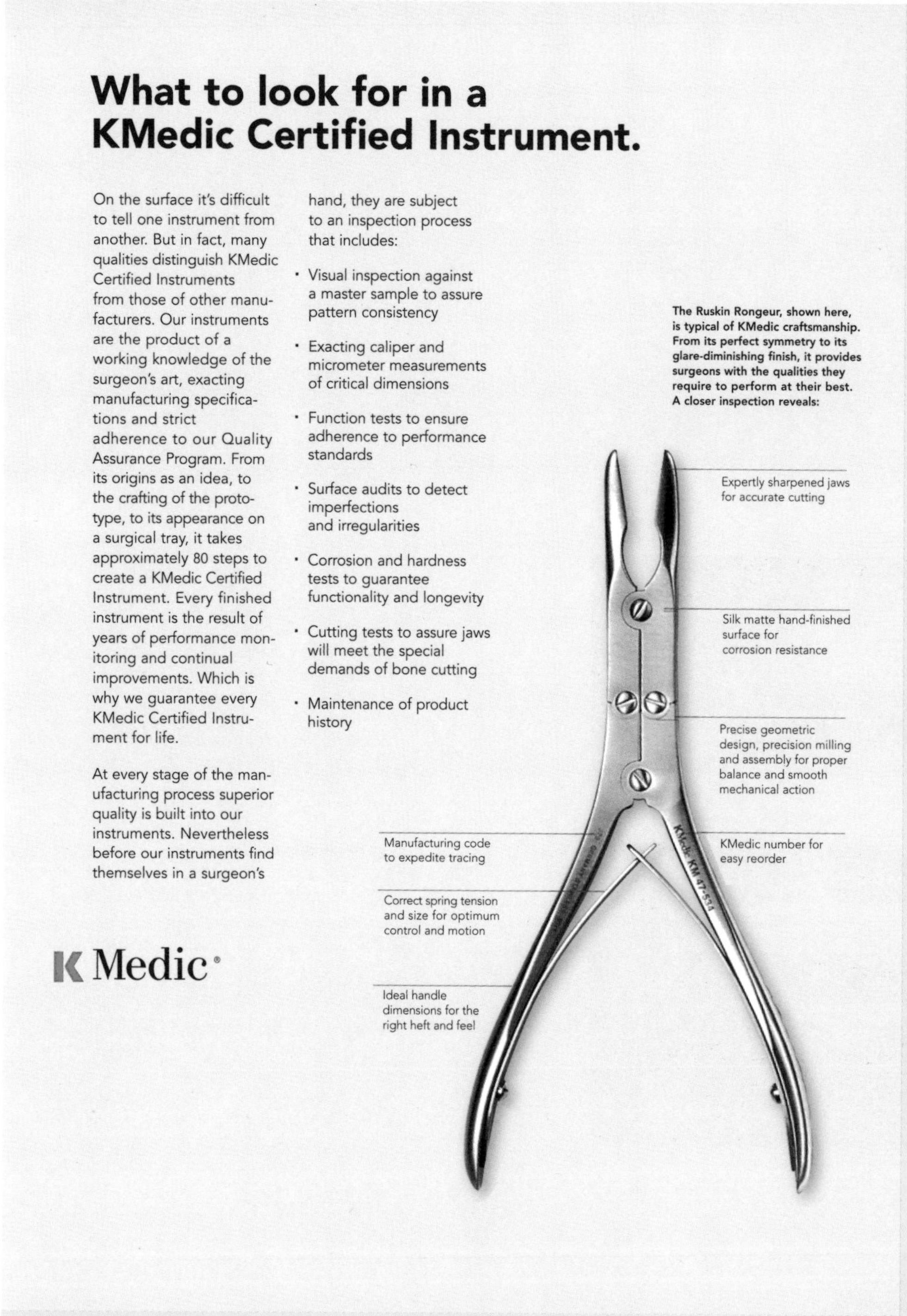

What to look for in a KMedic Certified Instrument.

On the surface it's difficult to tell one instrument from another. But in fact, many qualities distinguish KMedic Certified Instruments from those of other manufacturers. Our instruments are the product of a working knowledge of the surgeon's art, exacting manufacturing specifications and strict adherence to our Quality Assurance Program. From its origins as an idea, to the crafting of the prototype, to its appearance on a surgical tray, it takes approximately 80 steps to create a KMedic Certified Instrument. Every finished instrument is the result of years of performance monitoring and continual improvements. Which is why we guarantee every KMedic Certified Instrument for life.

At every stage of the manufacturing process superior quality is built into our instruments. Nevertheless before our instruments find themselves in a surgeon's hand, they are subject to an inspection process that includes:

- Visual inspection against a master sample to assure pattern consistency

- Exacting caliper and micrometer measurements of critical dimensions

- Function tests to ensure adherence to performance standards

- Surface audits to detect imperfections and irregularities

- Corrosion and hardness tests to guarantee functionality and longevity

- Cutting tests to assure jaws will meet the special demands of bone cutting

- Maintenance of product history

K Medic ®

The Ruskin Rongeur, shown here, is typical of KMedic craftsmanship. From its perfect symmetry to its glare-diminishing finish, it provides surgeons with the qualities they require to perform at their best. A closer inspection reveals:

Expertly sharpened jaws for accurate cutting

Silk matte hand-finished surface for corrosion resistance

Precise geometric design, precision milling and assembly for proper balance and smooth mechanical action

Manufacturing code to expedite tracing

KMedic number for easy reorder

Correct spring tension and size for optimum control and motion

Ideal handle dimensions for the right heft and feel

KMedic: What to Look for...
The feature that's important to a specific reader is the feature that should be important in the copy. The KMedic copy here mirrors the qualities of the product: Like the Kmedic instrument itself, the copy is purely functional. It doesn't distract or offer unnecessary information.

Creative Director/Writer   Robert Sawyer
Art Director/Designer   Dean Alexander
Design   Alexander Design Associates
Client   KMedic

I write for the good opinion of 200 people in this country.

George Hitchcock, in DURAK, The *International Magazine of Poetry*. No. 1, DURAK Press, 1978

Copywriters write for others, to others. But rarely are they given the opportunity to write to readers, to potential clients of their own choosing. Clients and products are assigned to them. And, if a copywriter doesn't write to the client's potential customer, the copy will likely fail, no matter how good the writing itself is.

Today's consumers are more sophisticated than yesterday's. They now resent obvious attempts at manipulation – attempts to sell them something they don't want or don't need. Two advertising professionals, Jonathan Bond and Richard Kirshenbaum in their book *Under the Radar*, tell how they built their New York City agency as a response to an 'epidemic of cynicism'. Their advertisements, including those for Kenneth Cole shoes and Target retail stores, are based on the proposition: the only effective method for reaching today's consumers is to go in 'under their radar'. In other words, to capture them without their knowing they've been captured.

So how do you write to people today who are resistant to a marketing message? How do you persuade them to give a little time to the message? You go in 'under their radar'.

Go in 'under the radar' by:
1. Treating readers like intelligent friends.
2. Writing to their hearts as much as their heads.
3. Having a conversation with them.
4. Not talking down to them.
5. Not wasting their time.

There is no such thing as a Mass Mind. The Mass Audience is made up of individuals, and good advertising is written always from one person to another. When it is aimed at millions it rarely moves anyone.

Fairfax Cone, founder, Foote, Cone & Belding, New York City, in John O'Toole, *The Trouble with Advertising…*, Broomall, Pa., U.S.: Chelsea House Publishers, 1981, p. 48

Read the best books first, or you may not have a chance to read them at all.

Henry David Thoreau (1817-1862), American philosopher, author, naturalist, 'A Week on the Concord and Merrimack Rivers' (1849), *The Writings of Henry David Thoreau*, Boston: Houghton Mifflin, 1906, vol. 1, p. 98

No one really listens to anyone else, and if you try it for a while you'll see why.

Mignon Mclaughlin (1915–), American journalist, *The Second Neurotic's Notebook*, Indianapolis: Bobbs-Merrill, 1966

know your **audience**

Design: Concrete Design Communications Inc., Toronto

Lounge.

Fossa

The Laughton Sofa series

KEILHAUER

Please contact Keilhauer for your nearest representative 1 800 724 5665.
www.keilhauer.com

Today's customers are resistant to blatant persuasion.

Today's customers are sophisticated.

Write only to a specific customer.

Go in 'under the radar' of the reader.

When executing advertising, it's best to think of yourself as an uninvited guest in the living room of a prospect who has the magical power to make you disappear instantly.

John O'Toole, *The Trouble with Advertising…*, 1981, Broomall, PA: Chelsea House Publishers, 1981

Keilhauer: Lounge
Sometimes it's better to say nothing or almost nothing. Keilhauer's potential customers are more interested in the lines of a sofa than the lines of copy. Here, the approach is show; don't tell. The advertisement's one word, 'Lounge', is rich and suggestive. It inspires feelings, not thought (see also pages 62 and 146).

Copywriter	John Pylypczak
Art Directors	John Pylypczak, Diti Katona
Photographer	Karen Levy
Agency	Concrete Communications Inc., Toronto
Client	Keilhauer

chapter **02**

elements
of copy

headlines

A headline may not be the first element seen in an ad – a picture claims that honour – but a headline is generally the first thing read. Therefore, if a headline fails to capture the reader's attention or, more to the point, the reader's interest, then the advertisement fails.

A good headline is never arbitrary.

A good headline has the power to catch readers' eyes when they're flipping through a magazine or newspaper, walking down the street, or opening the mail. But most of all, it has a purpose: to get readers to commit some of their time to the advertisement. They may find the visual beautiful, impressive, or even arousing, but the headline is the element which anchors the advertisement to reality and creates a context for everything else that follows.

The tone and manner of a headline must reflect the value or the positioning of a product or a brand. Except in rare cases, when irony or calculation is in play, the language should reflect the use and character of the product. If you pun or wordplay, have a very good reason for doing this. If the tagline under a logo is 'Let's Motor', a headline that reads 'Let's Park in Small Spaces' is consistent by every imaginable measure.

You may have discovered some curious facts about awareness and perception. This is one: at a party, the volume of background noise will generally drown out a conversation held only a few feet away. But if someone mentions your name or says something that's important to you, it gets your attention. In other words, you don't have to shout to be heard.

A headline that works:
1. Stands out.
2. Stops readers long enough for them to process the meaning.
3. Offers a promise, an invitation, or important news.
4. Persuades readers that it's worth their time to learn a little bit more about a product.

If it isn't riveting it doesn't matter what the body copy says.

Lionel Hunt, in *The Copywriter's Bible: How 32 of the World's Best Advertising Writers Write their Copy*, Hove, UK: RotoVision, 2000

An effective headline will grab the reader.

The language of a headline should mirror the character of a product.

A headline alone – without text – can get the job done.

A good headline offers an enticement to read what follows.

On average, five times as many people read the headline as read the body copy.

David Ogilvy, *Confessions of an Advertising Man*, New York: Ballantine Books, 1971, p. 92

Of course the last 50 years

have been a blur.

That's the whole point.

The 50ᵗʰ Anniversary Corvette.

Chevrolet and Corvette are registered trademarks and the 50th Anniversary Emblem is a trademark of the GM Corp. ©2002 GM Corp. Buckle up, America! ⚑ **corvette.com**

CHEVROLET 50 CORVETTE

<u>Chevrolet Corvette: 50th Anniversary</u>
Sometimes a headline is all you need. The 'Vette' here is about speed. It's about speed even when it's stuck in traffic or parked in a driveway. Therefore, you don't want to slow the reader down with copy. When you know what you are, the less you say, the more that's heard.

Creative Directors	Jim Gorman, Joe Puhy
Copywriter	Patrick O'Leary
Art Director	Marie Abraham
Account Executive	Mike Clayton
Production Supervisor	Kim Warmack
Agency	Campbell-Ewald
Client	General Motors Corp./Chevrolet Motor Division

Vanguard Group: How to Keep Sight of the Future...
This headline achieves something extraordinary. It brings up a painful truth and does it with a simple sleight of hand. It elicits a smile instead of a grimace. The headline persuades readers to believe that there's a solution to their anxiety. They don't have to read the text to feel this.

Copywriter	K. Wieden
Art Director	P Jervis
Art Producer	J. Thomas
Print Producer	R. Krieger
Account Management	T. Farnesi
Agency	Young & Rubicam NY
Client	Vanguard Group

Source: The Vanguard Group, Inc. Reprinted with permission.

Always be listening for headlines.

Jim Durfee, in *The Copywriter's Bible: How 32 of the World's Best Advertising Writers Write their Copy*, Hove, UK: RotoVision, 2000

I figured that if I said it enough [times], I would convince the world that I really was the greatest.

Muhammad Ali, former heavyweight-boxing champion, widely believed to be the greatest fighter of the 20th century: one of the most recognized and admired men in the world.

for a prospectus.
Corporation, Distributor.

Less talk.

There will always be more people who talk about doing something than who actually
do it. Our reputation is built on getting things done. Call 212 401 3500. **Make it happen.**

✳✳ RBS
The Royal Bank of Scotland Group

www.rbs.co.uk

RBS/Royal Bank of Scotland: Less Talk
This headline shows that it's possible to be direct and evocative at the
same time. It offers a simple proposition, and then goes on the
offensive. If you read only the two-word headline, you know that this
bank is about getting down to business.

Ex Creative Director/Copywriter	Simon Dicketts
Art Director	Fergus Flemming
Type Designers	Rob Wilson, Simon Warden
Photographer	Andy Green
Agency	M&C Saatchi
Client	Royal Bank of Scotland

body copy

Today's advertisements are not as copy heavy as yesterday's.

Look at advertising-club awards books from the 1980s to the early 1990s. You'll see a great many ads with long columns and heavy blocks of text. The presumption then was that factual information would influence decision-making. If you look at awards books and annuals today, you'll find a difference. There are now many advertisements with little or no copy. This suggests that either people are comfortable making decisions with fewer facts or that other factors have replaced their influence. Does this indicate that a cultural shift has occurred or that today's sparse copy is a passing fancy? The truth is, while award-winning work is always inspiring, it's also rarely relevant to the problems you will be asked to solve as a copywriter on an everyday basis.

There are products and relationships that require explanations. Conversely, there are brands that sell themselves. The most valuable lesson to take from all the work in the world of advertising today is that context is everything.

Even though Apple was successful with only two words – 'Think Different' – never assume that these two words just magically appeared in Apple's advertisements. In the development of every new concept, someone must build a narrative or create a scenario first. So even if you don't read or listen to a word, there are thousands of words behind every successful campaign. On the other hand, if your solution requires a headline that will whet a reader's appetite and body copy to satisfy it, then you'll have to sit down and write as simply and as clearly as you can.

What is the most absurd thing anyone has said to me about copy? That no one reads the copy. People read copy.

Richard Kirshenbaum, Kirshenbaum Bond & Partners, New York City, told to Robert Sawyer

Microsoft Windows xp Tablet PC Edition: 'Hand'
There's something to read everywhere in this double-page advertisement. The hand may be an unconventional surface, but who hasn't at one time written something on theirs, if only a telephone number? The headline is quiet, even possible to miss. The body copy is compact and descriptive, but almost hidden. It's the screen you want to read. The hand makes us smile, but it's the Tablet PC that makes sense. Together they tell the whole story.

Ex Creative Director/ Copywriter	Dar
Ex Creative Director/Art Director	Wa
Photographer	Ge
Agency	Mc
Client	Mic

There is no such thing as long copy. There is only too-long copy. And that can be two words, if they are not the right two words.

Jim Durfee, in *The Copywriter's Bible: How 32 of the World's Best Advertising Writers Write their Copy*, Hove, U.K.: RotoVision, 2000

What about interactive media?

Has the advent of interactive media changed the rules of copy? Yes and no. And, if it has, it's not as much as some people might claim. Bob Greenberg, chairman and CEO of the R/GA agency says, 'Copy isn't about words. It's about ideas and concepts. The visual metaphors we create have their basis in words.' He also believes that while there are now so many new ways to communicate, people still have to find a way to talk to one another.

Good body copy:

1. Says only what's important to say.
2. Addresses the prospective customer directly.
3. Uses as few words as possible.
4. Is honest and simple.
5. Sticks to the story.
6. Respects the product or service being promoted.
7. Holds the prospective customer in high regard.
8. Stops instantly when there's nothing more to say.

FIRST THINGS FIRST.

All online brokers are not the same.

Some offer advice. Others offer banking, lending and credit services. Some do all of the above. Not us. We're simply about trading. And if you're serious about trading, then that's good news for you.

The merger of Ameritrade and Datek makes us the nation's largest online brokerage, moving more online trades than any other.* It also centralizes the tools, information, value and support that traders use to make fast, educated, confident decisions.

No matter where you go for insight – your advisor, your online tools, or your gut – it makes sense to place your trade at Ameritrade.

Here's why:

2. ADVANCED ROUTING TECHNOLOGY.

You don't have milliseconds to waste. So Ameritrade works with multiple market centers, seeking best execution on your orders.* In fact, many of the trades placed through Ameritrade are directed to electronic market centers where buyers and sellers are matched, usually within seconds, without human intervention.

3. AMERITRADE'S COMMAND CENTER SCREEN.

Site navigation can be tricky and time consuming on some trading sites. Ameritrade's command center screen, however, integrates the tools you need to trade, on a single page. Tools like rapid order entry – which saves time by allowing you to

4. THE AMERITRADE® 10-SECOND GUARANTEE.

You know that speed is of the essence.* You want your trades executed quickly. So do we. That's why we will waive the commission on any qualifying internet equity trade that takes longer than 10 seconds to execute.* It's as simple (and reassuring) as that.

7. VALUE. $10.99 INTERNET TRADES.

$10.99 per internet equity trade, including stop and limit orders. If you think you're getting a higher-quality trade or better price improvement by spending more elsewhere, you haven't experienced Ameritrade trading.

8. GO WITH EXPERIENCE.

With the merger, Ameritrade is now the largest online trading firm in the industry, moving more non-professional or semi-professional trades than any other online broker.* We pioneered the first Internet trade in 1994. We've been working to put a greater share of investing power into the hands of the individual ever since. Join us. Get your share.

YOU'RE AN ACTIVE TRADER. YOU DEAL IN MILLISECONDS. GOT A MINUTE?

1. AMERITRADE STREAMER.™

Many online brokers offer streaming market data. Only Ameritrade gives you Streamer.® Originally developed by Datek, Streamer offers sophisticated tools that help you plot, measure and react to market nuances. Track up to 20 indices at once. Create new indices. View the most active stocks. Set alerts. View last sale on any stock. All for free. Plus, Level II Quotes and Streaming News are available for just a small extra charge.' Streamer. It's indispensable. And only Ameritrade has it.

enter orders with short text strings and a single click – streaming quotes, six indices, buying power, positions, balances and open orders.' All visible at once. All within reach.

5. AMERITRADE APEX.™

Active traders want powerful tools. At Ameritrade, if you average 10 trades per month over three months or maintain a $100K total account value, our Apex program gives you free access to Streamer Level II Quotes, free Streaming News (including access to the Business Wire,® Dow Jones Newswires™ and PR Newswire®) and a dedicated toll-free phone number to access Apex Client Services.'

6. OUTSTANDING 24X7 CLIENT SERVICES.

If you're an active trader, you know how important support is. If not, ask an active trader about client services at Ameritrade. They're no afterthought. They're at the core of everything we do. And (market holidays aside) they're there around the clock.

9. SIGN UP TODAY. GET 25 COMMISSION-FREE TRADES.

Right now, we'll give you 25 commission-free Internet equity trades when you open and fund an account.* Along with free Ameritrade Streamer, that's 25 opportunities to be convinced that Ameritrade is definitely the place for you to find your share.

25 COMMISSION-FREE TRADES
WHEN YOU OPEN AN ACCOUNT.

25 commission-free Internet equity trades. Free streaming data. Access to Level II Quotes. 10-Second Guarantee. 24-hour client services.

CALL 888 396 8002 OR GO TO
WWW.AMERITRADE.COM (OFFER CODE NOC)

AMERITRADE Ⱥ
What's your share?

Ameritrade: You're an Active Trader

If you have a great deal to say, it's a good idea to break up your story into digestible bites. By numbering sections, you can accomplish three things. First, two pages of copy are less intimidating than one. Second, readers can easily jump to whatever benefits they choose. Third, this structure will probably appeal to the target audience for this service, to people who both like and are good with numbers.

Creative Directors	Andy Berndt, Bill Oberlander
Account Handlers	Tina Cohoe, Michael Kelly
Agency	Ogilvy & Mather
Clients	Ameritrade

All rights in the copyrightable content and trademarks are owned and reserved by Ameritrade. Ameritrade® is a registered trademark of Ameritrade Holding Corporation.

You must make the product interesting, not just make the ad different.

Rosser Reeves, in Denis Higgins, *The Art of Writing Advertising: Conversations with Masters of the Craft* , Lincolnwood, ILL: NTC Business Books, 1990, p. 125

MAKES EVERYTHING ELSE SEEM A LITTLE TOO BIG.

Mini: Makes Everything Else...
Here is a sight gag with a punchline. The visual play forces a double take, but it's the body copy that gives meaning to this ad. The copy is interesting because it plays on the gag seriously. The simple sentence here – comprised of short words in two lines – is all that's necessary to deliver the message.

Creative Director	Alex Bogusky
Associate Creative Director	Andrew Keller
Art Director	Mark Taylor
Copywriter	Ari Merkin
Photographer	Daniel Hartz
Agency	Crispin Porter + Bogusky
	(Creative Dept Coordinator Veronica Padilla)
Client	Mini

Some products and services require explanations. Others sell themselves.

Apple used only two words: 'Think Different'.

A headline arouses. Body copy satisfies.

Simplicity is key.

Search for some way to relate the tiny, constricted world clients live in to the larger, sunnier world people actually care about. Deodorants aren't about keeping dry, they're about being loved. Computers aren't about getting more work done, they're about power. Cars aren't about transportation. Food isn't about hunger. Drink isn't about thirst. And so on.

Steve Hayden, in *The Copywriter's Bible: How 32 of the World's Best Advertising Writers Write their Copy*, Hove, UK: RotoVision, 2000

Martha Stewart Signature: Be True to Your Nature

A new product line from an established company is an opportunity both
to reinforce and to build on the brand name. The copywriter can remind
customers, already committed to a product, why they've remained
devoted. This is an opportunity also to make a big promise, because
customers expect you to. And why not be as enthusiastic as you are
informative? The copywriter's enthusiasm will give the potential
customer a reason to respond in kind.

Copywriter — Laurie Niehoff
Copy Director — Charlotte Barnard
Art Director — Susanna Ko
Deputy Creative Director — An Diels
Creative Director — Gail Towey
Agency — Created by an inhouse design team at Martha Stewart
Client — Martha Stewart Living Omnimedia

Reprinted by permission of Martha Stewart Living Omnimedia, Inc. © 2003 Martha
Stewart Living Omnimedia, Inc. All rights reserved.

Advertising is salesmanship mass produced. No one would bother to use advertising if he could [actually] talk to all his prospects face-to-face. But he can't.

Morris Hite, *Methods for Winning the Ad Game*, Dallas, TX.: E-Heart Press, 1988, p. 203

Our new one-person 401(k) works hard for your company's most important employee.

You.

There's a retirement plan that's right for you.

Prudential Financial offers a wide choice of retirement plans for self-employed individuals and small businesses, including the SEP, SIMPLE, or Keogh plan—and the one-person 401(k). Prudential can help you find out which plan is tailor-made for your particular business and your retirement goals.

You're an independent-minded entrepreneur, and you know the best way to run your own business. That's why you're the sole proprietor. But are you certain you've chosen the best way to fund your retirement? Prudential's new one-person 401(k) could be the perfect solution.

Contribute up to $40,000 annually, tax-deferred.

The one-person 401(k) allows a small-business owner (who has no employees) and a spouse to contribute as both owner and employee. So you're able to go beyond the maximum employee contribution of $12,000 and add up to $28,000 more as an owner.

A one-person 401(k) gives you flexibility.

Contributions are completely at your discretion—you can make higher contributions in good years and lower ones in off years. You can borrow against the plan without any tax penalty.

Keep more of your money growing, tax-deferred.

Because administrative requirements of the one-person 401(k) are greatly simplified, the cost of maintaining the plan can be significantly less. So the money you would have spent on maintenance fees is still yours.

Use the one-person 401(k)'s rollover possibilities.

You are allowed to roll over other qualified retirement plans and IRAs into a single one-person 401(k), making it that much easier to keep track of your assets.

Call today to learn how you can boost your retirement savings.

Ask for free information on one-person 401(k)s and other retirement plans that can help ensure your future.

1-800-THE-ROCK
ext. 3432   prudential.com

Advantages of Prudential's new one-person 401(k)

- Contribute up to $40,000 of income, tax-deferred, in 2003
- Contributions are discretionary
- Low costs keep more of your money growing
- Consolidate other retirement plans
- Take out loans without penalty and control repayment terms
- Choose from Prudential's comprehensive roster including stocks, bonds and mutual funds

---

Prudential Financial

Growing and Protecting Your Wealth®

Prudential Financial: Our New One-Person 401(k)...
Complex issues are best addressed in a logical manner. People are not in a hurry to give you their money, and so this advertisement doesn't rush. It progresses, step-by-step, from discussing the problems to offering a solution. Its tone is reasonable but has a measure of urgency. In a word, it's sincere. Little else is more persuasive than sincerity.

Copywriter   Colin McConnell
Designer   Bob Gary
Client   Prudential Financial

© 3/02 The Prudential Insurance Company of America. All rights reserved.

Taglines, slogans, and mottoes tend to be used interchangeably in the advertising business.

Normally taglines are found at the bottom of an ad and placed beneath or to the right of a brand name or a logo. More recently, taglines have been used as headlines, as body copy, and in various relations to the name. Some companies think they're unnecessary. Others believe they're a crucial part of their identity – important enough to trademark, service mark, or register. Sometimes these marks scream; sometimes they whisper.

Taglines are fragile entities and not particularly long lived. A shift in the business climate, the hiring of a new agency, the appointment of a new marketing director, the implementation of a new strategy – any of these changes can discharge one tagline and replace it with another. Taglines are generally developed by branding firms, generated by company employees, and written by copywriters.

Taglines are curious examples of writing. They obey no discernible rules of grammar and syntax. They are often the most eccentric element in an ad.

Taglines might appear:
1. In all-capital letters.
2. With only the first word capitalised, as complete sentences.
3. As sentence fragments.
4. Only rarely, as standard uses of good grammar – particularly when they incorporate periods, question marks, or exclamation points.

Taglines perform the following functions:
1. Complete the brand's story – act as the punchline to a joke.
2. Add an emotional element that confirms a relationship with the consumer.
3. Make an irrefutable argument for the brand.
4. Distill the brand's essence to remove any ambiguity or doubt.
5. Reiterate the brand's promise.
6. Close the deal.

A good tagline:
1. Is idiomatic or vernacular.
2. Consists of the fewest words possible.
3. Is concrete and specifically targeted to the audience.
4. Feels likeable.
5. Just sounds right and might even look as good on a tee shirt or a banner as it does in the best designed advertisements.

Taglines communicate the sum and substance of a company or a product.

For the launch in America of the Lifetime Television network – a name with no particular meaning – the tagline 'Women Are Watching' was written. The programming is for a female audience. The simple declarative sentence spoke volumes to three critical segments – advertisers, cable operators, and women – on whose indulgence the nascent network depended. On the other hand, when asked to position the SciFi TV network – a name that could not have been more descriptive, the same person wrote, 'Welcome to the Edge'. It chose to communicate a *double entendre*: the network's particular point of view and attitude and the fact that the programming was science fiction. When a new president was appointed at Lifetime, he replaced the line. When the SciFi network hired a new agency, the new one initially kept the line but, in due time, wrote their own. This sequence in the advertising business is the norm and to be expected.

The power of taglines becomes most evident when they leap off the page and enter popular discourse. Some taglines, like Nike's 'Just do it' or Apple's 'Think Different', have acquired a power that's almost scriptural.

Everyone talks about driving – 'Drivers wanted', 'Driving excitement', and so forth. [Crispin Porter + Bogusky] came up with the idea of 'Motoring' – and that felt right to us immediately. We also liked the phrase, 'Let's Motor', which became a nice way to lay the foundation for the brand. And this became part of the whole philosophy of what 'Motoring' represents. I also like the fact that we're saying, 'Let's motor', because that makes it inclusive, and the Mini brand has always been about inclusiveness.

Kerri Martin, marketing manager, Mini Cooper automobiles, in one. a magazine, The One Club for Art and Copy, vol. 6, no. 2, fall 2002

There is no such thing as conversation. There are intersecting monologues. That is all.

Rebecca West, in Robert I. Fitzhenry, *The Harper Book of Quotations*, New York: Harper Perennial, 1993, 3rd ed.

Here today. Gone tomorrow.

Some firms think taglines are important. Others don't.

Taglines often violate rules of grammar and syntax.

Talk to the reader; don't shout. He can hear you. Especially if you talk sense.

Tim Riley, in *The Copywriter's Bible: How 32 of the World's Best Advertising Writers Write their Copy*, Hove, UK: RotoVision, 2000

taglines

Some well-known taglines

The following firms and their taglines were selected at random. (The capitalisation and use of periods may not be that of the original.)

Review them from this perspective:
1. Analyse them alone, not within the context of an ad.
2. Ask yourself, 'Does the brand name and tagline together feel right and express a compelling idea?'
3. Keeping in mind that a tagline is a company's ultimate pitch, is the essence of the company all there, or is it absent?

Accenture	Innovation Delivered.
AIG	We Know Money.
American Century	Investment Managers.
American Express	Make Life Rewarding.^{SM}
ADP	We're the Business Behind Business.^{SM}
Aston Martin	Power, Beauty and Soul
Buick	The Spirit of American Style.
Callaway Golf	Enjoy the Game.™
Canon	Know How™
Chrysler	Drive & Love.
Cigna	A Business of Caring.
Cisco Systems	This Is the Power of the Network. Now.
DaimlerChrysler	Answers for Questions to Come.
Emerson	Consider It Solved.™
Expedia.com	Don't Just Travel. Travel Right.™
Fox News TV network	We Report. You Decide.™
GE	Imagination at Work.
HBO TV	It's not TV. It's HBO.
Hewlett Packard	HP Invent.
IBM ThinkPad®	Where the World's Most Innovative People Choose to Think.
Ikon	Document Efficiency at Work.^{SM}
Infinity	Accelerating the Future®
Jaguar	Born to Perform
Key Bank and Trust	Achieve Anything
Lexus	The Passionate Pursuit of Perfection
Liberty Mutual	It's More than Insurance. It's Insurance in Action
Macanudo	An American Passion
Microsoft	Your Potential. Our Passion
Morgan Stanley	One Client at a Time
NetJet®	Everything Else Is Just a Plane.^{SM}
New York Life insurance	The Company You Keep®
Nike	Just Do It
OnStar	Always There. Always Ready
Pfizer	Life Is Our Life's Work®
Phoenix	Wealth Management®
PSEG	We Make Things Work for You
TAG Heuer	What Are You Made of?
Tourneau	Since 1900.
UPS	What Can Brown Do for You?^{SM}
The Nature Conservancy	Saving the Last Great Places on Earth
The Vanguard Investment Group	In Our Way of Investing™
Time magazine	Join the Conversation
VeriSign	The Value of Trust.^{SM}
Xerox	The Document Company®
Yahoo!	Do You Yahoo!?

chapter **03**

Less is more.

…most compact full-featured notebook computer. U…
…a blazing G4 processor, super-crisp 12" display (1024…
…integrated Bluetooth. Plus a battery that lasts up to 5 ho…
…d into a stunning aluminum enclosure that's just 1…

writing
copy

s more.

...aturing a breathtaking 17" widescreen display, blazi...

...rDrive™ and the industry's first backlit keyboard. P...

...make it the most wirelessly connected notebook ev...

...s ultra-light and ultra-desirable. The new 17" PowerBo...

JEEP GRAND CHEROKEE OVERLAND

Redwood Burl trim | Sunroof | 10-disc CD changer | The most refined Jeep 4x4 | jeep.com/mag

ONLY IN A
Jeep.

NEVER CONFUSE YOUR NET WORTH
WITH YOUR SELF WORTH.

Jeep is a registered trademark of DaimlerChrysler Corporation.

Jeep: Never Confuse Your Net Worth…
If you can say exactly what needs to be said in a few words, then do it.
See how well it works in this advertisement that features a man and his
dog in the woods. In this context, anything less than writing on the level
of Ernest Hemingway would be a mistake. A good approach is to
separate the details from the headline, so that the thoughtful tone,
established by the headline, will not be disturbed by the details.

Copywriter	David Shih
Art Director	Paul Szary
Photographer	David Stoecklien
Agency	BBDO Detroit
Client	Jeep

David Abbott, in *The Copywriter's Bible: How 32 of the
World's Best Advertising Writers Write their Copy*, Hove,
UK: RotoVision, 2000

faith in words

**Getting the job done is central to good
copywriting.**

Good copy and good writing are not
necessarily the same thing. Copy has a
distinct purpose – to sell a product or a
service.

Writers tend to make the same mistake. That
mistake is a faith in words. Faith in their
ability to move the reader to care or – more
specifically – to move the consumer to the
cash register. Writers, as a group, harbour
the not-so-secret wish that words are the
magic element in a communication. And, it's
a wish that's often granted, provided the
writer has encouraged customers to read
what they've written, to believe it, and then
to act on the message.

The job of the copy in an advertisement is to
sell a particular product or service. And
getting this job done – selling a product,
service, or idea – is at the heart of good
copywriting. Writers indifferent to the sell will
never become successful copywriters. And
no matter what they write, it won't produce
an effective advertisement.

Good copy:
1. Focuses the reader's attention.
2. Conveys an idea.
3. Persuades the reader to believe that an
   idea is relevant.
4. Leaves the reader with a positive
   experience of the brand
5. Inspires a specific action.

Ten essentials behind writing good copy:
1. Focus on the work at hand.
2. Know your audience.
3. Keep it simple.
4. Be honest.
5. Make it passionate.
6. Keep current.
7. Write in a conversational, brief, and
   witty voice.
8. Serve as an advocate.
9. Express optimism.
10. Discard a 'brilliant idea' if it's not
    working.

Faith: A fidelity to a
promise you make;
sincerity with your
intentions; a firm belief
in something that cannot
be proven; something you
believe in, particularly a
strong conviction.

Indifference to the sell
will doom an advertisement
to failure.

If a copywriter isn't
positive and enthusiastic,
the reader won't be
either.

Know what to keep in your
preliminary copy and what
to throw away.

**Who's kidding whom? What's the difference between Giant and Jumbo?
Quart and full quart? Two-ounce and big two-ounce? What does Extra Long
mean? What's a tall 24 inches?**

Marya Mannes (1964), in Stephen Donadio, *The New York Public Library: Book of
Twentieth-Century American Quotations*, New York: Stonesong Press, 1992

Long copy has its uses – even if no one reads it.

Ken Segall, partner and worldwide creative director on Intel
account, Euro RSCG Worldwide, told to Robert Sawyer

There are so many reasons to own a Bose® Lifestyle® DVD system. And we've just added a new one.

Introducing the breakthrough ADAPTiQ™ audio calibration system.

Customizes sound to your room, so your Lifestyle® DVD system will sound best where it matters most. And it's only from Bose.

No two rooms sound exactly the same. Where you place your speakers, room size and shape, reflective and absorption qualities…even whether a room has rugs or hardwood floors can affect sound. And until now, there wasn't a simple way for home theater systems to account for these variables. Introducing the new ADAPTiQ audio calibration system, now available in Lifestyle® 35 and 28 DVD home entertainment systems. It listens to the sound in your particular room and automatically adjusts your Lifestyle® system to sound its best. So now, no matter what your room's acoustics, you'll enjoy action-packed movies and lifelike music delivered by a system performing to its fullest potential. ■ The ADAPTiQ system is just one reason you'll enjoy our Lifestyle® systems. Some others: An elegant media center with built-in DVD/CD player. Barely noticeable cube speakers. An Acoustimass® module that produces rich impactful bass. And an advanced universal remote that controls your system – even from another room. Bose Lifestyle® home entertainment systems. Now with the ADAPTiQ system, the height of our technology just got higher.

For a FREE information kit, or names of dealers and Bose stores near you call:
1.800.ASK.BOSE ext.E88   ask.bose.com/we88

Lifestyle® 35 DVD home entertainment system

BOSE®
Better sound through research®

Faith is an excitement and an enthusiasm: it is a condition of intellectual magnificence to which we must cling as to a treasure, and not squander on our way through life in the small coin of empty words, or in exact and priggish argument.

George Sand (1804–1876), French novelist, in a letter of May 25, 1866, translated from *Correspondence*, Paris: Calmann Lévy, 1883, vol. 4 (of 8)

The words which express our faith and piety are not definite; yet they are significant and fragrant like frankincense to superior natures.

Henry David Thoreau (1817–1862), American philosopher, author, and naturalist, 'Walden' (1854) in *The Writings of Henry David Thoreau*, Boston: Houghton Mifflin, 1906, vol. 2, p. 357

If you have abandoned one faith, do not abandon all faith. There is always an alternative to the faith we lose. Or is it the same faith under another mask?

Graham Greene (1904–1991), British novelist, Dr Magiot in *The Comedians*, New York: Viking Press, 1966, part 2, chapt. 4, sec. 4

An investment in safety at the point of care pays its own dividends.

There is a direct relationship between safety at the point of care and sound financial management. Technology that reduces medication errors at the critical point of administration can prevent injury and even death—adding new meaning to the phrase ROI.

ALARIS Medical Systems offers hospitals smart technology, tools and services designed to increase safety at the point of care; enterprise-wide systems that can be up and running quickly, with minimum disruption. Find out how cutting-edge technology means cutting-edge fiscal planning. To learn more, please call 1-800-482-4822.

ALARIS®
MEDICAL SYSTEMS

Medication Safety
at the Point of Care™

ALARIS Medical Systems, Inc. Worldwide Headquarters,
10221 Wateridge Circle, San Diego, California 92121-2772

Fax: 1-858-458-7760 | Customer Service: 1-800-482-4822
Website: www.alarismed.com

©2003 ALARIS Medical Systems, Inc. All rights reserved.

Alaris: An Investment in Safety...

On occasion you may be asked to sell the same product in different ads, to different audiences. In this case, don't try to identify what the various groups have in common, but rather, in each ad, focus on what's central to the experience of each party. Always speak to what's most pressing. For example when talking to an administrator, speak about saving money, and when writing to nurses, the quality of care.

Creative Director/Art Director	Dean Alexander
Creative Director/Copywriter	Robert Sawyer
Design Production	Paul Rodriguez
Design Firm	Alexander Design Associates Inc.
Account Directors	Peter Nolan, Dana Weissfield, Audrey Ronis-Tobin
Brand Marketing Specialist	Trudi Bresner
Agency	T. Bresner Associates
Client	Alaris Medical

Advertising is a future-
tense medium.

Eloquence is not enough.
Sometimes it's nothing.

Move from message to sale
quickly.

Few people admit to
getting ideas from
advertising.

Enlighten your reader. Educate them. Give them something for their time with you.

Copywriting always involves educating or re-educating your audience. You can't assume people know what you're going to tell them or that they will remember your last message – your last advertisement.

Every new message must offer something new. An advertisement can present an opportunity for you to talk to a new consumer. Or, at the very least, to talk to an old friend in a new way. This is because advertising exists in the future tense – an inescapable fact in a copywriter's life. Even the world's most-eloquent advertisement can never move a consumer to act instantaneously. The best that it might accomplish is to hurry along the process. But to the extent that copywriters can shorten the time between the message and the sale, then they have done their job well.

How do you teach customers something?
1. Know them well, inside and out.
2. Prepare a lesson plan.
3. Make the lesson exciting, new, and relevant.
4. Reward them for their attention.

The advertisements in a newspaper are more full of knowledge in respect to what is going on in a state or community than the editorial columns are.

Henry Ward Beecher, in Rhodas Thomas Tripp, *The International Thesaurus of Quotations*, New York: Thomas Y. Crowell Company, 1970, p. 18

I AM A SOYBEAN

I CAN BUILD YOUR NEXT

RECYCLED NEWSPRINT

CONSTRUCTION MATER

I HAVE THE PHYSICAL P

POWER TO MAKE A LOV

A SOYBEAN.

Convey genuine enthusiasm. I think that's important. If your reader senses you're excited by the product, there's a pretty good chance, he'll feel the same way.

Susie Henry, in *The Copywriter's Bible: How 32 of the World's Best Advertising Writers Write their Copy*, Hove, UK: RotoVision, 2000

educate. **re-educate**

E. I CAN BE MIXED WITH
ATE AN ECO-FRIENDLY
AVE THE POWER TO BE STRONG.
IES OF WOOD. I HAVE THE
FFEE TABLE. **I AM MORE THAN**

I AM A NETWORK.

I CAN BUILD INDUSTRIES FROM A BEAN. I CAN GIVE REAL-TIME INVENTORY UPDATES TO RETAILERS, MANUFACTURERS AND FARMERS SO NO BEAN IS WASTED. I CAN GUARD SOY SECRETS FROM ECO-FRIENDLY YET RUTHLESS COMPETITORS. I CAN USE THE POWER OF CONVERGED DATA, VOICE AND VIDEO TO TEACH A GLOBAL SALES FORCE ABOUT THIS VERSATILE LEGUME. I AM MORE THAN A NETWORK.

CISCO SYSTEMS

THIS IS THE POWER OF THE NETWORK. NOW.

cisco.com/powernow

<u>Cisco Systems: I am a Soybean</u>
Do soybeans talk? For that matter, do networks? When you ask people
to re-examine their assumptions, it's a good idea to approach the issue
from an angle they don't expect. Few people will admit that they get
their ideas from advertising. But this is no reason to stop introducing
new ideas to them. Do business people talk in parables? Yes, they have
for thousands of years.

Creative Directors	Dan Burrier, Gavin Milner
Copywriter	Steve P. Williams
Art Director	Justin Hooper
Photographer	Christian Stohl
Producer	Leslie D'Acri
Agency	Ogilvy & Mather
Client	Cisco Systems

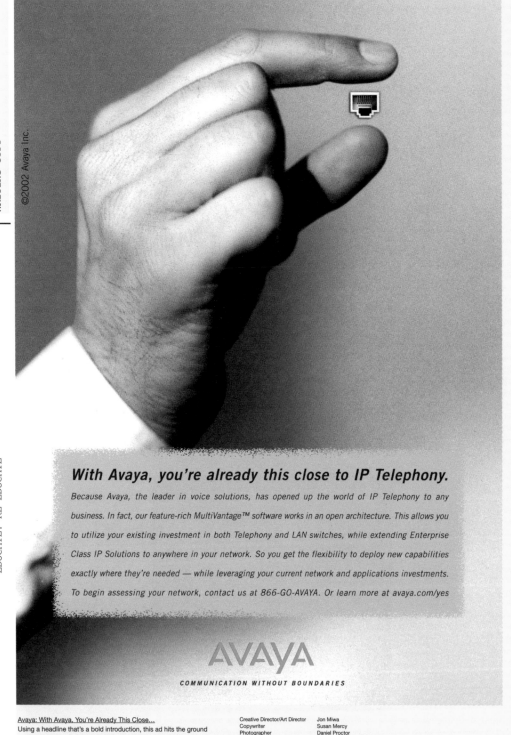

©2002 Avaya Inc.

With Avaya, you're already this close to IP Telephony.

Because Avaya, the leader in voice solutions, has opened up the world of IP Telephony to any business. In fact, our feature-rich MultiVantage™ software works in an open architecture. This allows you to utilize your existing investment in both Telephony and LAN switches, while extending Enterprise Class IP Solutions to anywhere in your network. So you get the flexibility to deploy new capabilities exactly where they're needed — while leveraging your current network and applications investments.

To begin assessing your network, contact us at 866-GO-AVAYA. Or learn more at avaya.com/yes

AVAYA

COMMUNICATION WITHOUT BOUNDARIES

Avaya: With Avaya, You're Already This Close...
Using a headline that's a bold introduction, this ad hits the ground running. It seems to know exactly what the reader needs. It makes claims and then expounds on them in a tone that feels more like speaking than reading. It begins with a promise and doesn't stop to catch its breath or let you ask a question. And, when it has said its bit, it stops. Just the way it should.

Creative Director/Art Director	Jon Miwa
Copywriter	Susan Mercy
Photographer	Daniel Proctor
Photo Rep.	Creative Management
Agency	FCB/SF
Client	Avaya

Education [is not] a discipline at all. Half vocational, half an emptiness dressed up in garments borrowed from philosophy, psychology, literature.

Edward Blishen (b. 1920), British author, *Donkey Work*,
London: Hamish Hamilton, 1983, part 3, chapt. 6

You can say the right thing about a product and nobody will listen. You've got to say it in such a way that people will feel it in their gut. Because if they don't feel it, nothing will happen.

William 'Bill' Bernbach, advertising pioneer, *Bill Bernbach Said…*, New York: DDB Needham Worldwide, 1989

Learning and teaching should not stand on opposite banks and just watch the river flow by; instead, they should embark together on a journey down the water. Through an active, reciprocal exchange, teaching can strengthen learning how to learn.

Loris Malaguzzi (1920-94), Italian educator, in Carolyn Edwards et al. (eds.), *The Hundred Languages of Children: The Reggio Emilia Approach to Early Childhood Education*, Westport, CT: Greenwood Publishing Group, 1993, chapt. 3

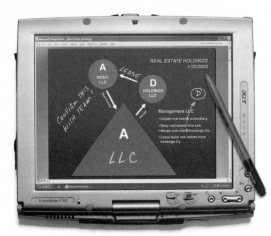

During lunch, in the park, a brainstorm.
It's a laptop. It's a simple pad and pen. It's a Tablet PC.

A great idea may not wait until you get back to the office, back to your desk. The Tablet PC puts the full power of Windows® XP Professional in a laptop computer that with a flip of the screen becomes as simple to use as a pad and pen. You write, draw, scribble, and erase directly on the screen. Plus it runs all of your favorite Windows XP compatible applications. So whether you're in your office or in a cab—the PC is more mobile, versatile, and powerful than ever before. For more information, visit microsoft.com/tabletpc

Microsoft **Windows** xp Tablet PC Edition

<u>Microsoft Windows xp Tablet PC Edition: 'Dirt'</u>
New products are less interesting than new solutions. In this ad, the first sentence of the headline creates a small drama familiar to all creative people – from businessmen to poets. And the second sentence describes the product's benefits with a takeaway message that's inescapable: buy this product, and you'll never lose an idea again. Here the sale is made in the headline; the details are in the body copy.

Ex Creative Director/ Copywriter	Dante Lombardi
Ex Creative Director/Art Director	Walt Connelly
Photographer	Geof Kern
Agency	McCann-Erickson SF
Client	Microsoft (Contact Pete Ryan)

A good ad should be like a good sermon: it must not only comfort the afflicted – it also must afflict the comfortable.

Bernice Fitz-Gibbon, *Macy's, Gimbels and Me: How to Earn $90,000 a Year in Retail Advertising*, New York: Simon and Schuster, 1967

Whose family?

The idea of 'family' is both real and imagined. Always more, and sometimes less, than what it seems. The idea of family challenges copywriters. They tend to rely on certain traditional values and what represents them. However, as a copywriter, you can incorporate new truths and practices. The effectiveness of your message will depend on how true it is to your readers' personal concepts of family.

Is it possible to write to a family? The answer is, 'No', if you believe that good copy is a conversation between two people.

Instead of writing to a family:
1. Chose one family member for the conversation.
2. Write to that person.
3. Persuade that person that your proposition is right.
4. Then permit that person to sell the idea to the rest of the family.

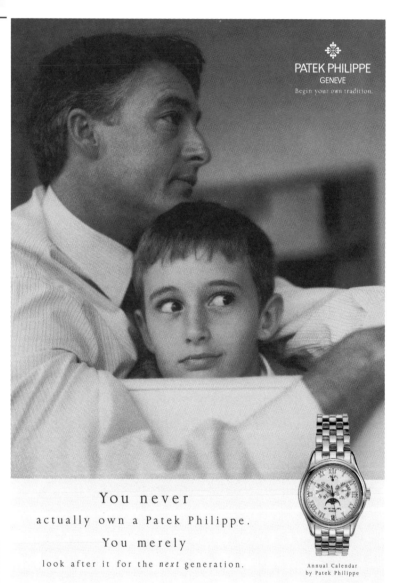

PATEK PHILIPPE
GENEVE
Begin your own tradition.

You never
actually own a Patek Philippe.
You merely
look after it for the *next* generation.

Annual Calendar
by Patek Philippe

Creative Director	Tim Delaney
Art Director	Warren Eakins
Copywriter	Tim Delaney
Photographer	Peggy Sirota (Represented by Eugenia Melian)
Agency	Leagas Delaney
Client	Patek Philippe

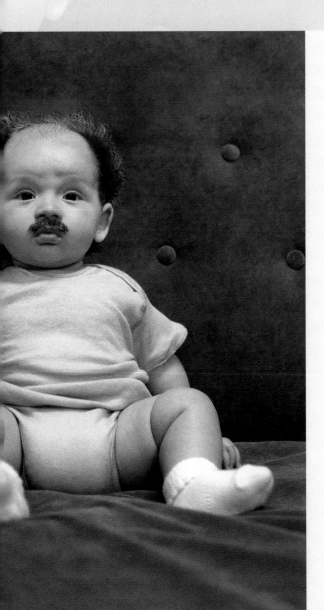

Adobe

He's got his father's eyes.

Want to give someone a brand-new hairdo? Now you can with Adobe Photoshop Elements 2.0, a program that's been optimized to run on an Intel® Pentium® 4 processor. Photoshop Elements gives you some of the same image-editing tools the pros use for less than $100.* It's fun, easy and undoubtedly the best way to give your mother-in-law that nose she's always deserved.

pentium 4

Adobe® Photoshop® Elements 2.0 | Tools for the New Work™

Adobe: He's Got his Father's Eyes
An advertisement about something appropriate for the home can call on images and metaphors about the family. In this case, a product associated with the workplace is re-imagined as something for the home. When using the family, it's important to avoid sentimentality, which this ad averts by having fun with a very tired but irrepressible cliché – something endearing about your child.

Creative Director	Rich Silverstein
Copywriter	Mike Sweeney
Art Director	Nancy King
Photograph	Heimo
Digital Artist	Mark Rurka
Print Producer	Suzee Barrabee
Engraver	Seven
Agency	Goodby, Silverstein & Partners
Client	Adobe Systems, Inc.

The idea of family is just that, an idea.

Call on new concepts of family. Discard the old ones.

Write to a person, not to the family.

Have a family member deliver the message to the others.

I think advertising is not only a form of education [but also] it's one of the most powerful forms of education in our society, and one of the reasons that it's so powerful is that it is not considered educational.

Dr Jean Kilbourne, author, filmmaker, advertising pioneer, in Sut Jhally (dir., ed., prod.), *Killing Us Softly 3: Advertising's Image of Women* video, 2000

Lincoln Aviator: Together We Will Rule the World...
Until recently, car advertising was directed only to men. Today, more and more ads are written to women. However, this example is gender neutral. Either a man or a woman might be saying what is in the headline. But it's not just about their individual concepts of the product. It's also about a shared view of the world – both want the power and luxury offered by this brand, and neither is willing to share them.

Creative Director/ Art Director	Sherry Pollack
Copywriter	Ernie Schenck
Graphic Designer	David Miazga
Art Buyer	Jessica Mirolla
Print Producer	Bea Alexander
Photography	Photo courtesy of Uwe Duettmann/ stocklandmartel.com
Agency	Young & Rubicam/Irvine
Client	Ford Motor Co. Lincoln Mercury Division

A TABLE IS NEVER *JUST* A TABLE.

OFFICE TABLES INNOVATED AND FABRICATED FOR THE WAYS PEOPLE REALLY USE THEM.

PRISMATIQUE
DESIGNS LTD.

1-888-414-7333   *TABLES THAT WORK.*   www.prismatique.com

Prismatique Designs: A Table is Never Just a Table
Did the writer conceive this scene? Maybe so, maybe not. But often before a single word is written, a story is developed, usually by the copywriter. In the advertisement here, the sell elements – plausibility and meaning – are built into the scenario. Even though the headline and body copy are very explicit, it's the story that makes the point: the advertiser designs furniture for how life is lived today.

Copywriter	Bruce MacDonald
Art Director	Jonathan Howells
Photographer	Chris Chapman
Agency	Dinnick & Howells
Client	Prismatique

One of advertisement's most brilliant accomplishments, to get us to believe that we're not affected by advertising.

Dr Bernard McGrane, Department of Sociology, Chapman University, Orange CA, in Harold Boihem (dir.), *The Ad and the Ego* video, STS Film Series, 1996

Performance. Unlike any other.

Born of a century of innovative engineering, even the most luxurious Mercedes-Benz offers unrivaled power and responsiveness. Call 1-800-FOR-MERCEDES. Visit MBUSA.com. **The S-Class**

Mercedes-Benz

Mercedes: 'Locomotive'
Performance. Unlike Any Other
This advertisement appropriates a number of obsolete notions about the rich by speaking about lineage in an understated, crisp tone. It's all tongue-in-cheek, but the reader will take away a message that's as clear as it is contemporary: the rich of today want to have their privileges and prerogatives, but they also want to have fun too (see also pages 16–17 and 118).

Copywriter	Sandy Mairs
Co-Creative Directors/Partners	Andy Hirsch, Randy Saitta
Art Directors	Andy Hirsch, Randy Saitta
Photographer	Darran Rees
Agency	Merkley + Partners New York
Client	Mercedes-Benz

Courtesy of Mercedes-Benz USA.

Money. It's just not what it used to be.

Tagline, Phoenix Wealth Management® advertising campaign

wealth

Today, even the establishment questions authority.

Approach the selling of a luxury item in the same way that you would any other product. After all, you won't be writing about abstract concepts but about objects and experiences. And people who buy luxury goods expect you to get to your point quickly – the faster the better.

Good copy should be appealing, bright, truthful, and sensible – no matter what it's selling. Aim for these qualities when you're selling expensive or rare things to the rich.

Engage yourself in a conversation with equals.

What to avoid:
1. Being affected.
2. Flattering the prospective customer.
3. Having archaic notions about money and class.
4. Feeling intimidated.
5. Thinking you're not just like them.

When selling expensive items, be aware that:
1. No one really needs what you're selling.
2. There is no shortage of beautiful or precious things.
3. Rich people are fully aware of points 1 and 2.
4. They are probably better informed on the subject than you are.
5. They have all the time in the world – but not for you.

Make your point fast.

Sell luxury in the same way as economy. Know your customer.

There's an abundance of precious objects out there.

Make believe that you, the copywriter, are the prospective customer.

At 60 miles an hour, the loudest noise in this new Rolls-Royce comes from the electric clock.

Renowned headline for a Rolls-Royce advertisement by David Oglivy, early 1960s

With the greater part of rich people, the chief enjoyment of riches consists in the parade of riches, which in their eyes is never so complete as when they appear to possess those decisive marks of opulence which nobody can possess but themselves.

Adam Smith (1723-1790), Scottish economist, *An Inquiry into the Nature and Causes of the Wealth of Nations*, Dublin: Whitestone, vol. I. xi. C. 31, 1776; edition of R. H. Campbell et al. (eds.), 1976

WRITING COPY

Patek Philippe: Who Will You Be...?
In this advertisement, nine simple words redefine the idea of luxury. The product has been transformed from a precious ornament into a symbol of a new kind of power. Notions of luxury and privilege are combined to suggest an extraordinary degree of freedom. It's an idea to appeal to a rich, contemporary woman for whom the trappings of wealth are no longer enough.

Creative Director	Tim Delaney
Art Director	Tim Delaney
Copywriter	Tim Delaney
Photographer	Regan Cameron
Agency	Leagas Delaney
Client	Patek Philippe

The people no longer seek consolation in art. But the refined people, the rich, the idlers seek the new, the extraordinary, the extravagant, the scandalous.

Pablo Picasso (1881–1973), Spanish artist, *Parade* magazine, January 3, 1965

The wretchedness of being rich is that you live with rich people... To suppose, as we all suppose, that we could be rich and not behave as the rich behave, is like supposing that we could drink all day and stay sober.

Logan Pearsall Smith (1865–1946), American essayist and aphorist, 'In the World' in *Afterthoughts*, London: Constable & Co., 1931

In writing advertising it must always be kept in mind that the customer often knows more about the goods than the advertising writers because they [customers] have had experience in buying them…

John Wanamaker, American department-store magnate

The rich are different from us.

F. Scott Fitzgerald

Yes, they have more money.

Ernest Hemingway

The Peninsula Group: Stay Focused
Wordplay, or verbal wit, is common in writing advertising because an entertaining text often disarms a reader's resistance. But the punning must not get in the way of the message, which in the case of this luxury hotel, is the promise that not only will your stay be comfortable, but you'll find everything you require to be productive (see also pages 88–89).

Creative Director	Lynn Kokorsky
Copywriter	Beth Levine
Photographer	Doug Menuez
Agency	AGENCYSACKS
Client	Peninsula Hotel Group

There are times when the dramatisation of facts to charm the reader will work very well. There are other times when being matter-of-fact – like giving instructions to a driver about how to find your house – will work as well.

Some copywriters object to a down-to-earth approach. They feel that the showmanship of similes and metaphors are at the heart of persuasive writing. Others choose to write pragmatically, objectively, even though they know they probably will not win industry awards.

But simple declarative statements work effectively for some products and strategies. Even so, straight talk does not have to be absent of subtlety. In fact, a simple advertisement is often the most difficult to write.

If you decide to take the practical, rational approach, start here:
1. Trust your reader's intelligence.
2. Make a long list of all the important points.
3. Shorten the list to only the essential details.
4. Cut the short list in half.
5. Then tell your story.

Keilhauer: This is Tom
When other chair manufacturers were selling sophistication through slick presentations, the creators of this advertisement decided to buck prevailing trends with a bit of humour and whimsy. The idea: simply introduce a new chair and then sell it. (When published in magazines, the page of 'This Is Tom' and the chair was placed on the right side, and the page of 'Tom Can Be Bought' and the logo appeared on the overleaf (see also pages 29 and 146).

Copywriter	John Pylypczak
Art Directors	John Pylypczak, Diti Katona
Photographer	Karen Levy
Agency	Concrete Design Communications Inc., Toronto
Client	Keilhauer

straight talk

Sometimes simple sentences
are best.

Talk that's straight can
also be subtle.

Communicating directly
insinuates honesty.

Advertising awards be
damned. Go for results.

tom
can be bought

Please contact Keilhauer for your nearest representative

1 800 724 5665

KEILHAUER

Clever words are not as good as straight talk.

Chinese proverb

Glenfiddich: The Independent Spirit

If you can distil the essence of your message into a few short sentences, then you've earned your salary. This headline refers both to the brand and to the consumer of the brand – a nice touch.

The copy is focused, tight, informative, and fast paced. The copywriter knows what's important to this company's potential customers and delivers it straight.

Photographer	Andrew Douglas
Agency	McCann-Erickson London
Client	William Grant & Sons Inc.

What I've learned over the years? That instinct discounts superlatives. That adjectives stretch credulity. That blatancy does not command respect. That overstatement creates resistance.

Tony Cox, in *The Copywriter's Bible: How 32 of the World's Best Advertising Writers Write their Copy*, Hove, UK: RotoVision, 2000

I want what I write to be rich with information. I want to be authoritative. So I try to learn everything I can about an account. I read everything I can find, talk to everyone I can. I research, research, research. I solve the problem to my satisfaction. Only afterward, do I write.

Beth Levine, copywriter, AGENCYSACKS, New York City, told to Robert Sawyer

They both work at the
same company.

Have the
same six-figure salaries.

So why is one looking forward to
early
retirement,

while the other looks forward to
the 15th and the 31st?

The difference is a Northwestern Mutual Financial Network Representative, offering expert guidance in retirement planning, financial services, and a network of specialists to help get you closer to all your financial goals.

Northwestern Mutual
FINANCIAL NETWORK®

Are you there yet?®

05-2010 ℗ 2003 The Northwestern Mutual Life Insurance Co., Milwaukee, WI

www.nmfn.com

Northwestern Mutual: They Both Work at the Same Company...
The issues addressed here are extremely complex, especially for women. Even so, the copy describes the situation and doesn't pull any punches. It's designed to be read quickly and understood completely. The copy strikes a nerve because its message is uncompromising: money is a zero-sum game; you either have it when you need it, or you don't.

Group Creative Director	Marcee Nelson
Copywriter	Rob Conrad
Art Director	Lars Larsen
Art Buyer	Christopher Grimes
Production Manager	Mary Beth Radeck
Traffic Manager	Jamila Lawrence
Account Management	Ron Schulman
Studio Technician	Tim Kalina
Agency	J. Walter Thompson/Chicago
Client	Northwestern Mutual Financial Network®

Rated The #1 Tasting Vodka In The World.

In 1998, the Beverage Testing Institute of Chicago conducted a blind taste test of more than 40 vodkas. They awarded points based on smoothness, nose, and most importantly, taste. Of all the vodkas, Grey Goose® Vodka emerged victorious, receiving 96 points out of a possible 100.

Founded in 1981, the Beverage Testing Institute conducts tests in a specially designed lab that minimizes external factors and maximizes panelists' concentration. The Institute selects judges based on their expertise, and its tasting and scoring procedures are widely praised as the best in the industry.

Score	Vodka
96	GREY GOOSE® VODKA
94	Canadian Iceberg Vodka
93	Stolichnaya Gold Vodka
92	Staraya Moskva Premium
91	Van Hoo Vodka
91	Stolichnaya Vodka
90	Tanqueray Sterling Vodka
90	Rain 1995 Harvest Vodka
89	Ketel One Vodka
88	Wyborowa Vodka
87	Kremlyovskaya Vodka
86	Finlandia Vodka of Finland
86	Alps French Vodka
85	Skyy Vodka
82	Original Polish Vodka
82	Glenmore Special
82	Fleischmann's Royal Vodka
81	Mr. Boston Vodka
80	Pole Star Vodka
80	Luksusowa Potato Vodka
80	Absolut Vodka
78	Cardinal Vodka
78	Barton Vodka
78	Barclay's Vodka
78	Amazon Vodka
76	Skol Vodka
74	Smirnoff Vodka
74	Crystal Palace Vodka
74	Belvedere
72	Schenley
69	Mr. Boston's Riva Vodka

NOTE: THIS REPRESENTS A SAMPLING OF THE 40 VODKAS TESTED
SOURCE: (BTI) BEVERAGE TESTING INSTITUTE INC.

www.greygoosevodka.com

Drink Responsibly.

To send a gift of Grey Goose® call 1-877-SPIRITS or visit www.877spirits.com. Void where prohibited.

WINNER OF THE PRESTIGIOUS WORLD SPIRITS CHAMPIONSHIPS

BEST NEW PRODUCT INTRODUCTION

Grey Goose: Rated the #1 Tasting Vodka in the World
When competing with brands that are iconic, there's little you can say that will make a noise. So why not let others say it for you? You can see this technique here, expressed with an almost journalistic impartiality. In fact, it relies so entirely on facts that it reads more like a news article than an advertisement.

VP Marketing	Bud Fenzel
Art Director	Bill Henderson
Copywriter	Deidre Maher
Client	Sidney Frank Importing Co., Inc.

**Don't talk of stars burning above.
If you're in love,
Show me!
Tell me no dreams filled with desire.
If you're on fire,
Show me!**

From the song 'Show Me', *My Fair Lady* musical play, by Alan Lerner and Frederick Loewe, published by Chappell & Co., Inc., © 1956

To make the best *Citron Martini* in the world, start with Grey Goose Le Citron.

Grey Goose Le Citron Martini

3 oz. Grey Goose® Le Citron
Garnish with a lemon twist

In 2001, the Beverage Testing Institute of Chicago conducted a blind taste test of the world's top lemon flavored vodkas. They awarded points based on smoothness, nose and taste. After careful consideration, Grey Goose Le Citron was rated the number one lemon tasting vodka. Praised for its "exceptionally smooth... medium body" and "very clean finish," Le Citron is the best tasting vodka in the world infused with the light zest of fresh lemon.

Rank	Vodka
1st	**GREY GOOSE® LE CITRON** ...Finishes very cleanly with an incandescent wash of ripe lemon flavor.
2nd	Stolichnaya Limonaya Vodka
3rd	Absolut Citron Vodka
4th	Tanqueray Sterling Citrus Vodka
5th	Ketel One Citroen Vodka

To send a gift of Grey Goose® call 1-877-SPIRITS or visit www.877spirits.com. Void where prohibited.   www.greygoosevodka.com
Drink Responsibly.

Grey Goose Le Citron: To Make the Best Citron Martini in the World...
To sell its lemon-flavoured vodka, Grey Goose again relies on the high praise it received from an independent source. The superlatives recited in this ad come from judges who conducted a blind taste test, not a copywriter's imagination. This approach is neither more nor less creative than an ad built on wordplay or endorsement. However, it does enjoy a big advantage by enabling the brand to literally show up its better-known competitors.

VP Marketing	Bud Fenzel
Art Director	Bill Henderson
Copywriter	Deidre Maher
Client	Sidney Frank Importing Co., Inc.

My mission is to make people feel first, so they can think, as opposed to making them think, so they can feel.

Baz Luhrmann in John Lahr, 'The Ringmaster' (Baz Luhrmann profile), *The New Yorker* magazine, December 2, 2002

Club 18–30

A sight gag by definition requires no words. If your idea is truly funny, all you have to do is raise an eyebrow, and your audience will get the punch line. The message here is as eloquent as it is highly targeted.

Creative Director	David Droga
Writer	Mike Sutherland
Art Director	Antony Nelson
Typographer	Scott Silvey
Photographer	Trevor Ray Hart
Agency	Saatchi & Saatchi/London
Client	Club 18–30

Words, words, words! They shut one off from the universe. Three quarters of the time one's never in contact with things, only with the beastly words that stand for them.

Mark Rampion (modelled on D.H. Lawrence), in Aldous Huxley (1894-1963), *Point Counter Point*, London: Chatto & Windus, 1928, chapt. 16

no **words.** or as **few** as necessary

Learn the difference between honesty and accuracy.

What part does a writer play in the creation of advertisements? Does he develop the concept? Create the scenario? Unfold the narrative? Today, headlines, body copy, taglines, captions, call-outs, and sidebars are merely elements of an advertisement's execution. And each one is optional. In a number of advertisements today, the visual 'tells' the story, in a manner that allows the audience to 'get' the message without the help of a word of copy.

Some copywriters claim the use of short copy is due to cilents' global reach today and, thus, to language barriers. Therefore, a universal visual idea can be understood by almost everyone everywhere. Others see new ways of ordering and processing information. Still others blame attention deficit disorder and functionally illiterate adults. And, they all may be right.

Will an emphasis on image alone diminish the writer's role? Not necessarily. In fact, it may be to the writer's advantage.

In theory, copy matters as much as it always has, but, today, it's coming at the consumer from another angle – the emotional (with images) rather than the intellectual (with words).

Image-based advertisements:
1. Remove a great deal of drudgery from the work.
2. Demand more intelligent ideas.
3. Require a writer to know more, to read more, to think harder.

The wickedest of all sins is to run an advertisement without a headline.

David Ogilvy, advertising pioneer, 'How to Write Potent Copy, 1, Headlines', *Confessions of an Advertising Man*, New York: Atheneum, 1984, p. 104

zoom-zoom

zoom-zoom

**Pitiless verse? A few words tuned.
And tuned and tuned and tuned.
It is good.**

Wallace Stevens (1879–1955), American poet, 'Gallant Château', *Ideas of Order*, New York: The Alcestis Press, 1935

zoom-zoom

www.mazdaUSA.com/newmazda6

For Nym, he hath heard that men of few words are the best men...

Boy, in William Shakespeare (1564–1616), *Henry V*, act 3, scene 2, l. 36–8

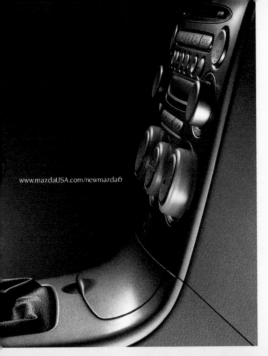

www.mazdaUSA.com/newmazda6

No-word advertisements can 'speak' a universal language.

Visual messages are immediate, direct, in your face.

Images call on the emotions rather than the intellect.

A brand name may be the only text required.

oom-zoom

azdaUSA.com/newmazda6

Mazda: Zoom-Zoom campaign
If you're appealing to your potential customers' emotions, use emotional language. If your concept is boys and their toys, 'Zoom-Zoom' is an articulate way to speak to their not-so-inner child.

Chief Creative Officer	John DeCerchio
Executive Creative Director	Michael Belitsos
Creative Director	Ken Camastro
Copywriter	Kip Klappenback
Art Director	Dennis Atkinson
Photographer	Bob Stevens
Agency	Doner
Client	Mazda

Let thy speech be short, comprehending much in few words.

The Bible, Old Testament, 'Ecclesiastes', 32:8

GRAFF

THE MOST FABULOUS JEWELS IN THE WORLD

721 MADISON AVENUE, NEW YORK NY 10021
TEL +1 212 355 9292 www.graffdiamonds.com

LONDON   NEW YORK   MONTE-CARLO   MOSCOW   DUBAI

Graff: The Most Fabulous Jewels in the World   Courtesy of Graff.
Fashion, luxury goods, and liquor advertisements generally use copy
sparingly or not at all. In these product categories, a company's name is
considered sufficient to convey the known brand's appeal or
advantages. However, when there is copy present, the words
differentiate the brand. Here the word 'fabulous', and all it implies,
positions this company.

Truthful words are not beautiful; beautiful words are not truthful.
Good words are not persuasive; persuasive words are not good.

Lao-Tzu (6th century B.C.), Chinese philosopher, in T.C. Lau (trans.),
Tao-te-ching, book 2, chapt. 81, New York: Viking Penguin, 1983

Less talk.

There will always be more people who talk about doing something than who actually do it. Our reputation is built on getting things done. Call 212 401 3500. **Make it happen.**

✲✲ RBS
The Royal Bank of Scotland Group

www.rbs.co.uk

RBS/Royal Bank of Scotland: Less Talk
Busy people don't have time to waste, especially when flipping through a magazine. Businessmen don't want to talk about their business. They want to get on with it. From a bank, they want financing to sustain or fuel an enterprise. This advertisement, which says very little, says what its prospects want to hear.

Ex Creative Director/Copywriter	Simon Dicketts
Art Director	Fergus Flemming
Type Designers	Rob Wilson, Simon Warden
Photographer	Andy Green
Agency	M&C Saatchi
Client	Royal Bank of Scotland

BRITISH AIRWAYS
britishairways.com

Flat, yes. Level playing field, no.

The truly flat bed in business class for a better sleep to London. It's almost an unfair advantage.

New Club World is available on most services between North America and London Heathrow.   ©2003 British Airways Plc

British Airways: Flat, Yes. Level Playing Field, No
Exclusion is the idea behind attitude. Not everyone will understand what
you're saying. And not everyone will get in, because not everyone is
sophisticated. The point of your copy should be to invite your reader
inside the exclusive circle. And, indeed, everyone wants to be inside
looking out.

Creative Director	Simon Dicketts/Matt Eastwood
Art Director	Bill Gallacher
Photographer	Richard Maxted
Agency	M&C Saatchi
Client	British Airways

with feeling or irony?

At one moment you'll be asked to write with feeling, the next moment with irony.

Good copywriters are aware of trends – of new ideas as well as new language usage. And copywriters should not resist being influenced by trends. Their agency bosses and clients will expect them to know about them, even insist they include them in their copy. Advertising, always transitory in nature, is even more transitory today, reflecting every new trend almost immediately after one appears.

Earlier generations of copywriters laboured over pinpointing a unique selling proposition and then polishing it until it was irresistible. They sold the facts, stretched them, coloured them, and put them in front of consumers' eyes. The prophets of the hard-sell – from Claude C. Hopkins to patrician David Ogilvy – fixed on one problem: how to sell.

Today, selling is just as important. But, now, copywriters sell the public's shared values – not a product's unique qualities.

It's time to accept that cool, as a signifier of meaningful rebellion, is belly-up in the water.

Rick Poynor, in *Obey the Giant: Life in the Image World*, London: August; Basel: Birkhäuser, 2001

project **attitude**

Guidelines for writing with attitude:
1. Use the slang of the prospective customer.
2. Emphasise exclusivity and scarcity.
3. Know that yesterday's kitsch may be today's good taste.
4. Be arrogant if it feels right.
5. Assume a savvy, specifically targeted demeanour.
6. Engage the prospective customer's shared ideas of social acceptance.
7. Call on clichés only when you manipulate then anew.

Less is more.

…most compact full-featured notebook computer. Unlike other compact notebooks, …e a blazing G4 processor, super-crisp 12" display (1024 x 768), slot-load CD-burning/DVD-…integrated Bluetooth. Plus a battery that lasts up to 5 hours, so you can do more – anywhere. …d into a stunning aluminum enclosure that's just 1.2" thin. The new 12" PowerBook.

More is more.

Presenting the world's first 17" notebook computer. Featuring a breathtaking 17" widescreen display, blazing 1GHz G4 processor, slot-load CD/DVD-burning SuperDrive™ and the industry's first backlit keyboard. Plus AirPort Extreme (802.11g) and integrated Bluetooth make it the most wirelessly connected notebook ever. All miraculously engineered into a 1"-thin enclosure that's ultra-light and ultra-desirable. The new 17" PowerBook.

Attitude
An assumed pose, posture, stance, air, demeanour, comportment, presence. Example: 'Her attitude made me think she was rich, but she wasn't.'

Slang
Language peculiar to a particular group; an informal non-standard vocabulary composed typically of coinages, arbitrarily changed words, and extravagant statements. British example: 'The dinner was brilliant', meaning 'good' not 'intelligent'. American subculture example: 'Got some dead presidents?', meaning 'Do you have any money', based on the images of deceased US presidents that appear on paper money.

Irony
The use of words to express something other than, and especially, the opposite of the literal meaning. Examples: 'Your father will be pleased when he sees your school grades!', meaning the father will not be pleased with the bad grades, and 'Nice hairdo you've got there!' meaning it's strange or unattractive.

Cliché
A commonplace, banal, prosaic, overused expression, one having lost its effectiveness or impact through overuse; especially maxims. Examples: 'Don't put the cart before the horse', and, particularly, 'Avoid clichés at all costs'.

MOTOHIPNOTIZA

Motorola: Moto campaign
As the nature of communication evolves, what sounds right is right. Because targeted groups of people you want to reach are becoming narrower and narrower segments, it's imperative to know their slang. When you know it, then you sling it. Talking their talk is half the job of projecting attitude.

Creative Director	Miguel Muñiz
Art Director	Raúl Espino
Copywriter	Rodrigo Puga
Photographer	Platon
Producer (Art Buyer)	Leslie D'Acri
Agency	Ogilvy, Mexico City Office
Client	Motorola

Concerning the advertising campaign for New York restaurant Florent: *The first pieces we did for Florent were only advertised in Paper magazine. We wanted it to be the cool restaurant, so we designed the ads with no address, no telephone number, no American Express cards. If you didn't know somebody who knew [about the restaurant], you were out of it.*

Tibor Kalman (1949-1999), formerly principal, M&Co, New York City, in Peter Hall, *Tibor Kalman: Perverse Optimist*, New York: Princeton Architectural Press, 1998, p. 66

Concerning an advertisement for Booker's Bourbon:
We gave a guy who spent $50 on a bottle of bourbon something to talk about.

Mike Lescarbeau, creative director, One and All agency, Minneapolis,
told to Robert Sawyer

Heller Ehrman v. Conventional Thinking

If a truer symbol of the archetypal lawyer exists, may it stand up and be known. At Heller Ehrman you won't find heavily starched attorneys thinking equally rigid thoughts. Instead, you'll find teams of spirited individualists looking beyond the expected to the exceptional, where the extraordinary solutions are found.

Heller Ehrman
ATTORNEYS

Challenging the laws of convention.™

Heller Ehrman: Heller Ehrman v. Conventional Thinking
One way to get your prospect's attention is to go on the offensive. Attack what you're not, and spell out what you are. Set the terms of the argument. The tone here is aggressive and decidedly uncompromising. It demands the prospect to choose: the competitors or us, the past or the future. Throw down the gauntlet! It's the essence of attitude.

Copywriter	Jody Horn
Art Director	Gregg Foster
Photographer	Chris Wahlberg
Agency	Publicis USA
Client	Heller Ehrman

**Above their scrap of history,
Only an attitude remains…**

Philip Larkin (1922-1986), British poet, in 'An Arundel Tomb' in John Lehmann (ed.), *The London Magazine*, vol. 3, no. 5, London: Chatto & Windus, 1956

…oday's smartest advertising style is tomorrow's corn.

…lliam 'Bill' Bernbach, advertising pioneer, *Bill Bernbach Said…*, New York: DDB …edham Worldwide, 1989

A little bit town and country. A little bit rock and roll.

*The charm and manners of the British. With a propensity to get down. Behave accordingly.
Take high tea in a bikini. Spend the day at the yacht club – the night at
the jazz club. It's paradise, with a pedigree. Conveniently located two hours from New York.*

1.800.225.6106 ~ www.bermudatourism.com ◢|BERMUDA

ROLEX

Worth a second glance, even when you know the time.

Oyster Perpetual in stainless steel

FOR THE NAME AND LOCATION OF AN OFFICIAL ROLEX JEWELER NEAR YOU, PLEASE CALL 1-800-367-6539. WWW.ROLEX.COM

Rolex and Oyster Perpetual are trademarks.

…muda Department of Tourism: A Little Bit…

…er your readers, but be careful. Know what their emotional buttons …and push them. Today lines of taste are blurred and crossed with …nity. The taste of yesterday isn't tasteful today. Now, sophistication …mix of high and low culture. You have to know both to get it right.

Creative Director
Art Buyer
Copywriter
Photographers:
Couple
Golf shadow
Blue fish
Bathing Suit
Agency
Client

Jean Byers
Catherine Johnson
Michelle Gusman

Anne Menke
Ian Macdonald-Smith
National Geographic stock
Martyn Thompson
Arnold Worldwide
Bermuda Department
of Tourism

Rolex: Worth a Second Glance…

When products become icons, the idea of function becomes secondary to the pleasure of owning them. So, if you're selling a watch today, you're not selling a better timepiece or even precious jewellery. In the 1980s, people thought about status, in the 1990s, about good taste. But, today, you have to offer something that's both real and abstract. Or, in a word, offer attitude (see also page 187).

With thanks and acknowledgement to Rolex.

All products of a certain type conform more or less to the same standards as others. They are all designed the same way, made with the same technology, and essentially perform the same. Nevertheless, a copywriter's task is to give consumers a good reason to buy the product assigned to the advertising agency to advertise, no matter the product's sameness.

Copywriters often claim that they are taking this or that approach to make a product special. That what they are doing will make people stand up and take notice. That people will talk about the advertisement. Of course, creative people propose, and then reality disposes – wishful thinking is one thing, but the result is everything.

However, here is one way to help your product stand out: make an emotional connection with your audience.

How to create emotion:
1. Identify with a prospective customer's already-extant passion.
2. Use emotional words or those that evoke emotions, such as 'dream'.
3. Be aware that the evocation of emotion can be a powerful tool.
4. Assume that people want to be stimulated, even excited.
5. Have a chat, and don't lecture.
6. Talk to the prospective customer, not about the advertiser.
7. Be friendly and even risk intimacy.

we see
the toughest reservation in town.
Where there are big ideas but still small budgets, we see opportunities for success. That's what inspires us to create software that helps small businesses start, grow, and thrive. Even the smallest companies get a chance to compete on today's tech-driven playing field. microsoft.com/potential
Your potential. Our passion.

BISTRO

Microsoft®

Mircosoft Corporate: 'Bistro'
The audience of an advertisement has dreams. And often clients have the means to turn those dreams into reality. The job of a copywriter is to bring them together. Does the small businesswoman or female entrepreneur believe that giant Microsoft cares for her? She will if the tone and manner of the writing accurately reflect her vision and passion.

Ex Creative Director/Copywriter	Dante Lombardi
Ex Creative Director/Art Director	Walt Connelly/Ashley Reese
Photographer	Kiran Masters
Agency	McCann-Erickson SF
Client	Microsoft (Contact: Peter Cohen)

The intellect is always fooled by the heart.

François de La Rochefoucauld (1613–1680), French author and moralist, Richard I. Fitzhenry (ed.), *The Harper Book of Quotations*, New York: Harper Perennial, 1993, 3rd ed.

get **emotional**

zoom-zoom

You grab hold of it.
And vice versa.

Introducing the all-new 220-hp MAZDA6
You wrap your hand around the short-throw, 5-speed leather-wrapped shifter. Finding first, you feel the potent 220-hp engine launch you cleanly from the line. As you continue climbing through the gears, the sport-tuned double-wishbone front suspension lets its talents be felt. And as one twisty stretch of road leads to another, the same thought keeps running through your mind. "Is it me that won't let go or the other way around?" The all-new MAZDA6 sports sedan. Drive it. You'll know.

Well-equipped $19,050*
220-hp V6 model shown $23,115*
*MSRP excludes tax, title, license and emissions fees.

mazda
www.MazdaUSA.com/newMazda6

Mazda: You Grab Hold of It...
People want to be excited. They want emotional involvement. They want to feel passionate about things around them. A copywriter is in the unique position to give words to these feelings, as the writer did in this ad, which isn't so much about loving your car as having an affair with it.

Chief Creative Officer	John DeCerchio
Executive Creative Director	Michael Belitsos
Creative Director	Ken Camastro
Copywriter	Kip Klappenback
Art Director	Dennis Atkinson
Photographer	John Marion
Agency	Doner
Client	Mazda

All products in a specific category are essentially the same.

A copywriter's promised results and the actual results may be very different.

Many products, like fashion, are less about function than emotion.

Everyone has wishes waiting to be satisfied.

Make it illogical for the reader not to believe.

Tom Thomas, in *The Copywriter's Bible: How 32 of the World's Best Advertising Writers Write their Copy*, Hove, UK: RotoVision, 2000

some students dream
of staying after school

Because those students are part of Agilent After School, a global program where real Agilent scientists and engineers volunteer their time to demonstrate how much fun science really can be. It's a balloon-powered car. An actual operating periscope you can build at home. It's how a light bulb turns on. It's igniting a spark in tomorrow's scientists and engineers. And it's just a small part of Agilent's ongoing efforts to enrich communities the world over.

www.agilent.com

Agilent Technologies
dreams made real

Agilent Technologies: Some Students Dream…
Certain words, in a particular context, can assume a power to transcend their everyday usage. One of these words is 'dream'. When it's juxtaposed with a black child in a classroom, as here, the word becomes inextricably linked to the American civil-rights leader Dr Martin Luther King: 'I have a dream'. When your copy taps into a desirable social force, it can acquire power and relevance.

Creative Directors	Mark Canavan, Mark Reichard
Copywriter	Chris Lozen
Art Director	Steve Miller
Photographer	Blaise Hayward
Agency	McCann-Erickson
Client	Agilent Technologies, Inc.

Reprinted with permission from Agilent Technologies, Inc. Permission to use the photograph comes from Karen Pinsky, Corporate Advertising Director.

Directness has its place in advertising but so do subtlety and obliqueness.

David Abbott, in *The Copywriter's Bible: How 32 of the World's Best Advertising Writers Write their Copy*, Hove, UK: RotoVision, 2000

The majority of advertising is either invisible or bad. We strive for work that people notice, like and talk about. Work that creates a buzz.

Staff, Boone Oakley agency, Charlotte, North Carolina, U.S., in *one. a magazine*, The One Club for Art and Copy, vol. 6, no. 2 (Fall 2002)

Write to people's hearts as well as their heads. That's where most decisions are made.

Alfredo Marcantonio, in *The Copywriter's Bible: How 32 of the World's Best Advertising Writers Write their Copy*, Hove, UK: RotoVision, 2000

Phoenix Wealth Management: Unaccustomed
This is a striking ad for a number of reasons but foremost for its extraordinary honesty. One word, 'Powerless', makes it impossible to ignore. Richard Kirshenbaum has said: 'If you want your work to be current, put current events in your work.' This writer has, and the result is an ad that could not be more timely…or more persuasive.

Agency: Cossette Post Communications
Client: The Phoenix Companies, Inc.

Donna Karan: Hosiery
Very few words, like in this example, can accomplish more than merely identifying the brand or describing the product. Fashion photography is less about showing details than about eliciting an emotion. The copy here centres on a single word, 'ultimate', and the feelings and images that 'ultimate' provokes.

Creative Director	Trey Laird
Art Director	Hans Dorsinville
Photographer	James Houston
Agency	Laird + Partners
Client	Donna Karan

[Good copy has a] subtle, powerful sell, which is enveloped in intelligence, honesty, wit and charm.

Dean Hacohen, copywriter, Lowe & Partners/SMS, New York City

He valued emotion – not for itself, but because it is the only final path to intimacy.

E.M. Forster (1879–1970), British writer, *The Longest Journey*, Edinburgh: W. Blackwood and Sons, 1907, part II, chapt. 18

The most beautiful emotion we can experience is the mystical. It is the power of all true art and science. He to whom this emotion is a stranger, [someone] who can no longer wonder and stand rapt in awe, is as good as dead.

Albert Einstein (1879–1955), German physicist, in Philipp Frank, *Einstein: His Life and Times*, New York: Alfred A. Knopf, 1947, chapt. 12, sec. 5

eBay Electronics: The Word Plasma Excites You
People want to communicate, not be lectured to. The voices copywriters choose depend on many factors, ranging from strategies they've developed specifically for individual advertisements to ones they always speak with. This copy addresses the reader directly, as if the writer knows the reader on a first name basis. There's a good reason for this informality. It says to the reader: 'We're talking to you, not about us'.

VP Consumer Marketing eBay	Gary Briggs	Dir. Acct Management	Robert Riccardi
Sr Director Brand Marketing	Annette Goodwine	Account Director	Brian McPherson
Sr Brand Marketing Manager	Steve Reinhardt	Account Manager	Yasmina McCarty
Manager, Brand Marketing	Kim Vostermans	Asst. Account Manager	Kim Lewis
Brand Marketing Specialist	Serena Shnayer	Agency	Goodby, Silverstein & Partners
Creative Director	Jamie Barrett	Client	eBay
Art Director	Michael Kennedy		
Copywriter	Lionel Carreon	eBay is a trademark of eBay Inc.	
Digital Artist	Will Hung		
Photographer	Dan Escobar, San Francisco		
Producer	Max Fallon		

A copywriter is always writing to someone. So when you sit down to write, imagine that you're initiating a conversation with a new friend. There is, however, one big difference between a social chat and an advertisement. An advertisement is never simply a way to pass time. You're ultimately asking your friend to consider spending some hard-earned cash. Whether the product is a new soft drink, discounted airfare, or a flat-screen TV, you are brokering a sale. And, in the best of all possible worlds, your new friends will believe that the reason you are telling them about a product is because you genuinely believe it will add something of value to their lives.

When writing to a friend, do:
1. 'Talk' in a tone that's the most appropriate to the occasion.
2. Share information you believe is valuable.
3. Be engaging throughout.
4. Express respect.
5. Share.

When writing to a friend, don't:
1. Rely on the headline alone.
2. Be boring or bored.
3. Exclude content from form.
4. Assume they are listening.
5. Patronise or condescend.

FABRICA   © Benetton Group spa 2003

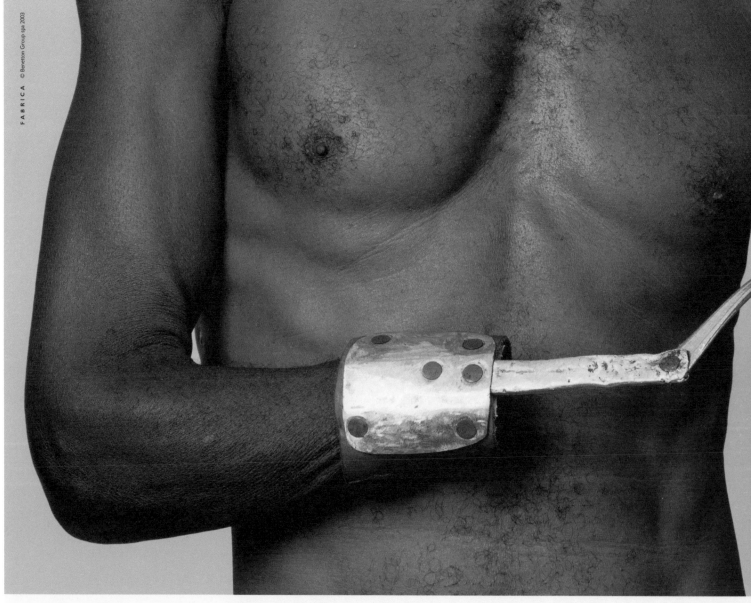

ALL ABOUT YOU

CHAPTER 03

KISS & SELL

United Colors of Benetton: Food for Life
There are opportunities to write to people without addressing them directly. In this case, a larger or meta-message is delivered: 'What's ultimately important to you, is also important to us.' In this way, a more genuine connection is made that transcends the typical consumer/advertiser exchange.

Copywriter	Amy Flanagan
Photographer	James Mollison
Agency	Fabrica
Client	Benetton Group S.p.A.

© 2003 Benetton Group S.p.A.

all about **you**

In addition to selling individual products, advertising teaches all of us to be, above all, consumers. It teaches us that happiness can be bought, that there are instant solutions to life's complex problems, and that products can fulfill us, can meet our deepest human needs.

Dr Jean Kilbourne, author, filmmaker, advertising pioneer (presenter) and Sut Jhally (director, editor, producer), *Killing Us Softly 3: Advertising's Image of Women* video, 2000

Pull people aside. Address them directly and intimately.

Have a conversation with a 'friend'.

Believe the product or service is truly beneficial.

Ask yourself, is the message boring?

The prospect is more important than the product.

John Bevins, in *The Copywriter's Bible: How 32 of the World's Best Advertising Writers Write their Copy*, Hove, UK: RotoVision, 2000

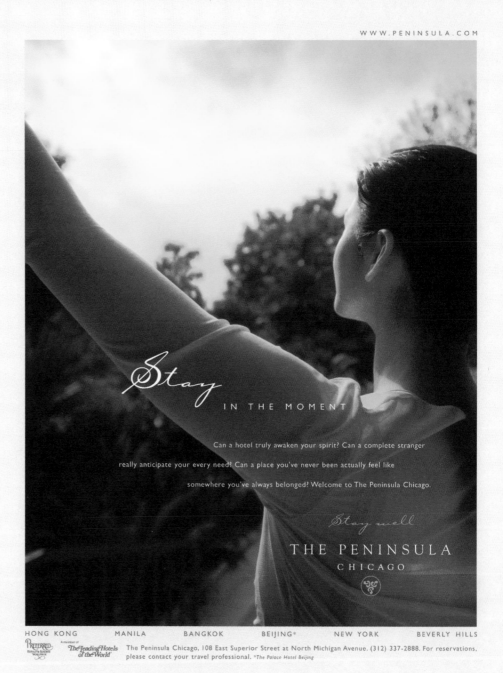

The Peninsula Group: Stay Who You Are
When writing to an older, more accomplished, or affluent person, the copywriter should understand that this person's expectations are a function of experience, expertise, and taste. In these circumstances, refrain from simply listing information. Instead, try to connect on a deeper, more personal level. The prospective customer will appreciate it (see also page 61).

Creative Director	Lynn Kokorsky
Copywriter	Beth Levine
Photographer	Doug Menuez
Agency	AGENCYSACKS
Client	Peninsula Hotel Group

I am one who believes that one of the greatest dangers of advertising is not that of misleading people, but that of boring them to death.

Leo Burnett, *100 Leo's*, New York: McGraw-Hill, 1965, p. 18

About the advertisement for Mitsubishi automobiles:
For the demographic we're trying to reach, we have to be authentic. We're edgy, we take risks, but we don't do it for the sake of it. Our car, our brand is about how it makes you look and feel.

Greg O'Neill, president/chief operating officer, Mitsubishi Motor Sales North America, in *Creativity* magazine, May 2003

The sacred is found boring by many who find the uncanny fascinating.

Mason Cooley (b. 1927), American aphorist, *City Aphorisms*, Third Selection, New York, 1986

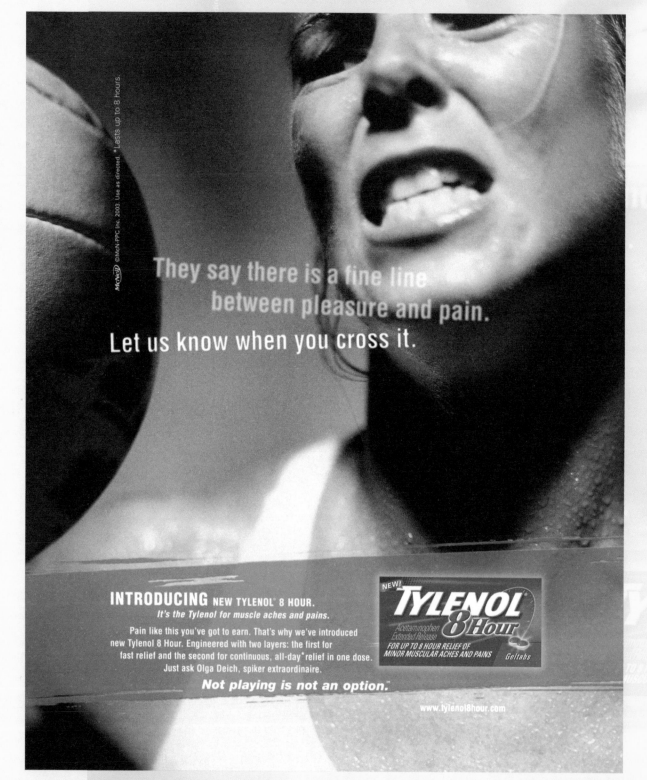

They say there is a fine line
between pleasure and pain.
Let us know when you cross it.

INTRODUCING NEW TYLENOL® 8 HOUR.
It's the Tylenol for muscle aches and pains.

Pain like this you've got to earn. That's why we've introduced
new Tylenol 8 Hour. Engineered with two layers: the first for
fast relief and the second for continuous, all-day*relief in one dose.
Just ask Olga Deich, spiker extraordinaire.

Not playing is not an option.

NEW!
TYLENOL
8 Hour
Acetaminophen
Extended Release
FOR UP TO 8 HOUR RELIEF OF
MINOR MUSCULAR ACHES AND PAINS   Geltabs

www.tylenol8hour.com

Tylenol 8 Hour: They Say There Is a Fine Line...
An advertisement that says, 'I know you', has to have the story down
pat. Any inconsistency, inaccuracy, even a little stretching of the facts
will be read as insincere. Here the writer not only hit the right note –
tough and vulnerable – but added a layer of authenticity with the
unexpected endorsement at the bottom.

Creative Director	Lee St. James
Copywriter	Muffy Clarkson
Art Director	Hamish McArthur
Photographer	Sandro, Sandro, Inc.
Agency	Saatchi & Saatchi
Client	McNeil

© Nestlé

Your day.

Your way.

Sure, sometimes life spins out of control. But the rich roast flavor and aroma of Taster's Choice₀ coffee makes it easy to stay on top of things. So you can handle whatever's in your path.

www.TastersChoice.com

Advantage You.™

<u>Taster's Choice: Your Day, Your Way</u>
Is it presumptuous for an ad to suggest it knows you? Not if the tone is convincing and empathetic and delivered with a bit of humour. Here the voice sounds like a friend's, one who not only knows what the prospective customer is experiencing but one who is sharing a way to get through it.

Creative Director	Richard Mahan
Copywriter	John Sullivan
Art Director	Pieter de Koninck
Photographer	Mark Laita
Illustrator	Mark Busacca
Agency	McCann-Erickson
Client	Nestlé

© Nestlé is a registered trademark of Nestlé S.A.

Advertising is what you do when you can't go see somebody. That's all it is.

Fairfax Cone, advertising pioneer and founder, Foote, Cone and Belding, in James B. Simpson, *Contemporary Quotations*, Binghamton, N.Y.: Vail-Ballou Press, 1964, p. 84

WHAT
YOU DREAM
IS WHAT YOU GET

DESIGNED BY **ECCO** for use by:

AT&T

HTC

Orange

Oxygen

Microsoft

Siemens

T-Mobile

and others

E | C

C | O

ECCO Design
Strategic Product Innovation

New York
212.989.7373
info@eccoid.com
www.eccoid.com

ECCO Design: What You Dream is What You Get
Business-to-business and retail consumer advertising are increasingly
indistinguishable. This ad addresses business prospects as if they were
retail consumers, and the decision to buy hinges on their dreams.
On the other hand, the writer hasn't forgotten what sells – a list of Blue
Chip clients makes an age-old promise: 'You're judged by the company
you keep'.

Copywriter	Dev Patnaik
Art Director	Bryan Lee
Creative Director	Eric Chan
Photographer	Ken Skalski
Agency	ECCO Design
Client	ECCO Design

**Talk to consumers about cars and they rarely talk about the things car
companies talk about. They talk about what image they want to project
through their cars; which one is me [they ask]?**

Eric Hirshberg, executive creative director, Deutsch Advertising, New York City,
in *Creativity* magazine, May 2003

Promise, large promise, is the soul of an advertisement.

Samuel Johnson (1709-1784), British author and lexicographer (*The Idler*, no. 40, Universal Chronicle, London, January 20, 1759), reprinted in W.J. Bate et al. (eds.), *Works of Samuel Johnson*, New Haven: Yale Edition, vol. 2, 1963

promises. **promises**

Promise
A stated commitment by someone to do or not do something specified; a reason to expect something that is positive.

Expectation
A look forward to or anticipation of something, particularly a pleasurable expectation; a visualisation of a future event or situation.

Desire
A conscious feeling about wanting something that promises enjoyment or satisfaction.

Need
A condition when you think you require a supply of or a relief from something.

Almost 250 years ago, Samuel Johnson made his observation about the promise being the essence of advertising. And nothing has changed since, although the nature of the promise has become considerably more complex. One source of the complication is the various governmental agencies that have passed regulations to curb certain claims. Another is the threat of challenges to promises by competitors. But the most significant source comes from consumers themselves.

What consumers want from a product or service often transcends the limits of objective benefit. Numerous benefits, often described as 'intangibles', are expected from products. There are expectations that cars can go beyond the actual distance per gallon, food will provide fewer calories per servings, and TV create more laughs per episode. Some of them are reasonable, even measurable – for example, the prestige associated with particular automobiles. But others are more abstract and concern the ineffable depths of human yearning. As a writer, you will be expected to find words for them.

Traditional measurable promises
M&M's
Melt in Your Mouth, not in Your Hand
Avis
We're No. 2. We Try Harder
Dial
Aren't You Glad You Use Dial?
Don't You Wish Everyone Did?
Crest
Look, Ma, No Cavities!
Rice Crispies
Snap, Crackle, and Pop

Transitional Promise
Volkswagen Beetle
Think Small

Contemporary abstract promises
IBM
Can You See It?
Infiniti S²UV
People Will Talk
Accenture
Innovations Delivered
Intel
Unwire
Expedia.com
Don't Just Travel. Travel Right

Now a promise made is a debt unpaid, and the trail has its own stern code.

Robert W. Service (1874-1958), Anglo-Canadian poet, from 'The Cremation of Sam McGee', line 33, in Margaret Atwood (compiler), *New Oxford Book of Canadian Verse in English*, New York: Oxford University Press, 1983

Promise is most given when the least is said.

George Chapman (trans.), *Homer's Batrachomyomachia-Hymns and Epigrams, Hesiod's Works & Days, Musæus' Hero & Leander, Juvenal's Fifth Satire*, London: John Russell Smith, 1858

Never promise more than you can perform.

Publius Syrus (42 B.C.), a Roman slave, in D. Lyman (trans.), *The Moral Sayings of Publius Syrus*, Cleveland, Ohio, U.S.: L.E. Bernard & Co., 1856, Maxim 528

WestLB: Spectacular, Isn't It?...
Financial advertising is closely regulated by governments, limiting what can be promised. The conversation in this headline is a play on financial performance, which suggests results rather than guarantees. The language, which is as generic as it is careful, explains what someone can expect. But the tone throughout is surefooted and confident.

Agency   Ogilvy & Mather GmbH & Co. KG
Client   WestLB AG

The man who promises everything is sure to fulfil nothing, and everyone who promises too much is in danger of using evil means in order to carry out his promises, and is already on the road to perdition.

Carl Gustav Jung (1875-1961), Swiss psychiatrist, 'After the Catastrophe' (1945), in William McGuide (ed.), *The Collected Works of C. G. Jung: Civilization in Transition* (Bollingen Series No. 20), Princeton, NJ, U.S.: Princeton University Press, 1970, vol. 10, para. 413

Promises are the uniquely human way of ordering the future, making it predictable and reliable to the extent that this is humanly possible.

Hannah Arendt (1906-1975), American political philosopher, 'Civil Disobedience', *Crises of the Republic: Lying in Politics, Civil Disobedience on Violence, Thoughts on Politics, and Revolution*, New York: Harcourt Brace Jovanovich, 1972

We Bring Fanatical Support™ to Managed Hosting.

Too many companies view customer service as a necessary evil. At Rackspace, the service we provide our customers is our competitive advantage. We care about and understand the importance of keeping your business running smoothly. That's the beginning of Fanatical Support.™

Fanatical Support™ is more than simply solving problems for customers. Fanatical Support™ is having expert Level 3 Technicians, not an automated attendant, answer your calls 24 hours a day. It's about a team of systems, network, and security engineers who are dedicated to immediately responding to your support needs. It's about all these things and a lot more.

To get a Fast Quote
888.571.8961
www.rackspace.com/fastquote

rackspace
MANAGED HOSTING

450 servers.

12 storage platforms.

3 operating systems.

27 nightly backup schedules.

And that's just one office. Monitor and manage all your storage from a single point with BrightStor Portal.

You're burning the midnight oil. So is your storage network. And the only things growing faster than your storage needs are your storage problems. The solution? BrightStor™ Portal. A breakthrough in enterprise-wide storage software that provides a single point of management. With a flexible portal interface that's easy to use, BrightStor Portal gives you a customized view of your entire storage environment so you can respond to any issue, anytime, anywhere. In-depth access to business-critical information 24 x 7 will help you simplify operations, increase productivity and maximize cost efficiency across your enterprise. Hey, with more and more issues under control, you may actually get to go home. ca.com/brightstor/portal

BrightStor™ Storage Solutions   Computer Associates®

© 2003 Computer Associates International, Inc. (CA) All rights reserved.

<u>rackspace: We Bring Fanatical Support...</u>
In the light of today, the word 'fanatical' in this headline is a curious choice that most companies would eschew. But this company has embraced its implications. 'Fanatical' isn't just a word taken from a thesaurus. It defines the client's promise of customer service. In fact, the client feels strongly enough about 'Fanatical Support' to trademark the phrase.

With thanks and acknowledgement to rackspace.

<u>Computer Associates: 450 Servers...</u>
A promise is pointless when it's been conjured by a copywriter who doesn't understand a customer's problem. This is why the writer of this advertisement has gone to great lengths and exactness to demonstrate his understanding of her potential customer's needs. As a result, the reader doesn't need a great leap of faith to believe that the solutions promised here will be kept.

Creative Director/Copywriter	David Dircks
Associate Creative Director/	
Art Director	Laura Caggiano
Account Manager	Rob Dircks
Photography	The Image Bank, Getty Images
Agency	Dircks Associates
Client	Computer Associates

'Consumer culture' refers to culture characterised by omnipresent advertising and the penetration of the techniques of advertising into all realms of human life, including our self-images and identities.

Sandra LaFave, West Valley College, in 'Marxism and its Critique of Consumer Culture', classroom outline/guide, West Valley College, Saratoga, CA., U.S.

Coming soon: clothes that talk to washing machines. Because nob likes a shrunken sweater. More intelligence at motorola.com

intelligence Ⓜ

Motorola: Home appliances campaign

The technology is anything but simple. The implications are certainly profound. But in an industry that had a habit of breaking its promises, understatement equals credibility. The idea of the reader eavesdropping on a conversation between objects is both entertaining and informative. These advertisements talk to consumers, manufacturers, and even people in government. The subject is our shared future. And who doesn't want to be part of that conversation?

Creative Directors	Bill Oberlander, Dan Burrier
Art Directors	Jeff Curry, John LaMacchia
Copywriters	Jeff O'Keefe, Andrea Sinert
Photographer	James Day
Producer (Art Buyer)	Leslie D'Acri
Agency	Ogilvy NY
Client	Motorola

Talking about oneself can also be a means to conceal oneself.

Friedrich Nietzsche (1844-1900), German philosopher, quote from *Oxymoronica: Paradoxical wit and wisdom from history's greatest wordsmiths*, by Dr Mardy Grothe, New York: HarperResource (an imprint of HarperCollins) 2004

understatement. or a **big** idea **simplified**

Understated copy can be straightforward, or it can involve some play. But it is always quiet by design.

Understatement is not about demonstrating a product's superiority. Nor is it about grabbing headlines. Or announcing a time-sensitive offer. The inherent lack of pressure in an understated approach frees you as the copywriter to focus on your message. At its best, understatement allows you to tell your client's story in a simple, honest and, most importantly, unobtrusive way.

The use of understatement is a popular technique because it can be employed in several ways:
1. When you want to whisper your promise.
2. When a knowing remark is sufficient to communicate your message.
3. When asking the reader to think about something in an unexpected way.

The successful use of understatement requires:
1. Confidence in the product and its promise.
2. The courage not to be all things to all people.
3. Faith that the copy can tell your story.

In the prime, often-cited understatement, Corneille's heroine continues to love Rodrigue, even though he killed her father, and says the affirmative by negating its opposite:
Go, I hate you not. (Va, je ne te hais point.)

Pierre Corneille (1606-1884), French playwright, Chimène in *Le Cid* (1637), Paris: Larousse, 1965, act 3, scene 4

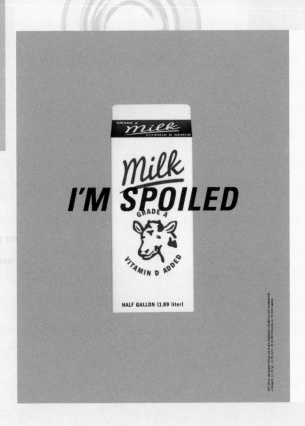

Soon, your fridge will know when the milk goes bad. And order more, just in time for breakfast. More intelligence at motorola.com

intelligence **Ⓜ** everywhere

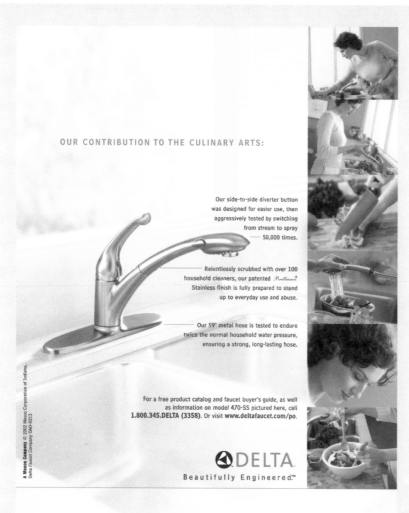

OUR CONTRIBUTION TO THE CULINARY ARTS:

Our side-to-side diverter button was designed for easier use, then aggressively tested by switching from stream to spray — 50,000 times.

Relentlessly scrubbed with over 100 household cleaners, our patented *Brilliance* Stainless finish is fully prepared to stand up to everyday use and abuse.

Our 59" metal hose is tested to endure twice the normal household water pressure, ensuring a strong, long-lasting hose.

For a free product catalog and faucet buyer's guide, as well as information on model 470-SS pictured here, call **1.800.345.DELTA (3358)**. Or visit **www.deltafaucet.com/po**.

A Masco Company © 2002 Masco Corporation of Indiana, Delta Faucet Company DAD-0213

◇ **DELTA**
Beautifully Engineered.™

Delta: Our Contribution to the Culinary Arts
This modest headline conceals an interesting strategy – a tap isn't a fitting, it's a kitchen utensil. However, if you made too loud a point of it, you'd open it to debate. Stated quietly, it's a reasonable, if not compelling, claim. While the text lists important benefits, what sells this product is that the voice speaks to cooks. And cooks love gadgets and utensils.

Creative Director	Cindy Sikorski
Copywriter	Cristina Lorenzetti
Art Director	Bill Biliti
Account Executive	Chris Adams
Production Supervisor	Craig Rinkel
Agency	Campbell-Ewald Advertising
Client	Delta Faucet

Simplicity, simplicity, simplicity! I say, let your affairs be as two or three, and not a hundred or a thousand; instead of a million count half a dozen, and keep your accounts on your thumb-nail.

Henry David Thoreau (1817–1862), American philosopher, writer, and naturalist. Walden, 'Where I Lived, and What I Lived For', *Walden; or, Life in the Woods*, Boston: Ticknor and Fields, 1854

WINDOW OFFICE

CORNER OFFICE

OVAL OFFICE

Allen Edmonds
For All Walks of Life™

Styles from business to casual, sizes 5-16 and widths AAA-EEE. Truly th widest selection available. And with our Recrafting® process, they'll be read for a second term. For a catalog and dealer near you, call 1-800-235-234
Made in USA   *Shoes from top to bottom: Halsted, Hillcrest, Byron*   *allenedmonds.co*

Allen-Edmonds: Window Office. Corner Office. Oval Office
Bill Oberlander, a creative director at Ogilvy & Mather advertising in New York City, claims, 'Capture the eye, then the heart, and the brain will follow'. Perhaps this is why wit is rare in fashion advertising. But this copy is not only clever; it conveys a great deal of information. To shoe-literate men, this advertisement speaks about variety. Here, the voice of a mentor in the clipped manner of a colleague offers invaluable advice to young men who aren't sure of what to wear. ('Oval Office' refers to the U.S. President's office.)

Sr VP Executive Creative Director	Mike Bednar
Sr Art Director	Matt Herrmann
Sr Copywriter	Sandy DerHovsepian
Agency	Cramer-Krasselt
Client	Allen-Edmonds

Simplicity is a strict taskmaster.

Mason Cooley (b. 1927), American aphorist, *City Aphorisms*, New York: Ninth Selection, 1992

Simplicity is an acquired taste. Mankind, left free, instinctively complicates life.

Katharine Fullerton Gerould (1879–1944), American writer, *Modes and Morals*, New York: Charles Scribner's Sons, 1920, chapt. 3

Understatements don't have to be plain.

Simple is never simple.

Understatements can create the illusion of honesty.

Speak softly.

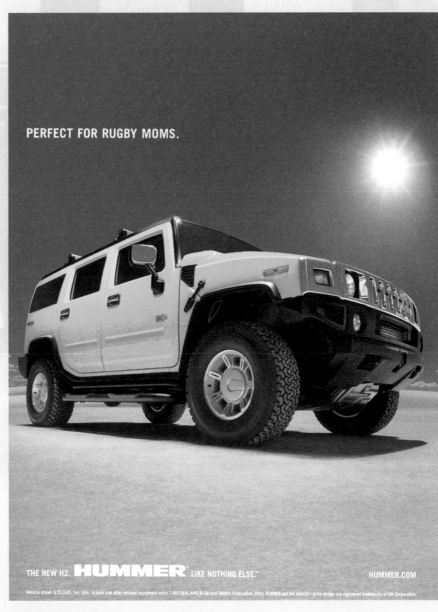

PERFECT FOR RUGBY MOMS.

THE NEW H2. **HUMMER** LIKE NOTHING ELSE.™   HUMMER.COM

Vehicle shown $50,545. Tax, title, license and other optional equipment extra. 1-800-REAL-4WD © General Motors Corporation. 2003. HUMMER and the vehicle's grille design are registered trademarks of GM Corporation.

HUMMER: Perfect for Rugby Moms

This vehicle shouts. Drivers who want to go unnoticed don't drive a HUMMER. But with a deft touch of irony, a potential driver's resistance is softened by the suggestion that this vehicle is just a bigger, tougher SUV. The copy makes its point in a friendly, understated way; stays perfectly with the brand; and still reaches for the potential female customer.

Creative Directors	Lance Jensen, Gary Koepke
Art Director	Will Uronis
Copywriter	Shane Hutton
Photography	Tim Simmons
Agency	Modernista!
Client	HUMMER (Div GM)

2003 General Motors Corporation.
Used with permission of HUMMER and General Motors.

Good advertising is built on a strong concept, consistently played before the right audience.

Tom Murphy, former writer/creative director, J. Walter Thompson and Bozell, New York City, told to Robert Sawyer

I sent the club a wire stating, 'Please accept my resignation. I don't want to belong to any club that will accept me as a member.'

Groucho (Julius Henry) Marx (1890-1977), American comedian and actor

WRITING COPY

JOIN US

CHAPTER 03

KISS & SELL

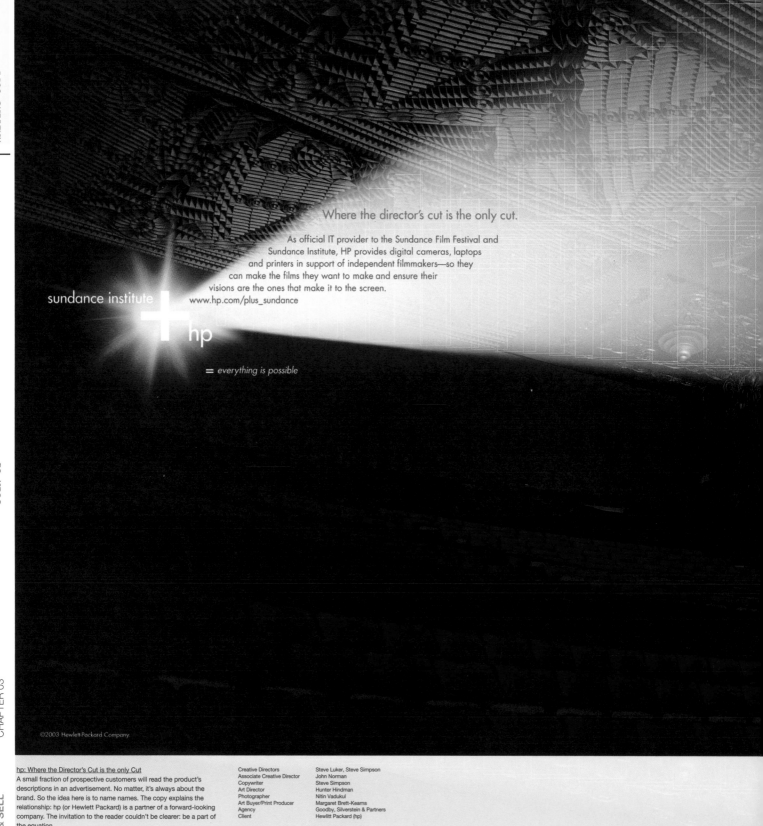

Where the director's cut is the only cut.

As official IT provider to the Sundance Film Festival and Sundance Institute, HP provides digital cameras, laptops and printers in support of independent filmmakers—so they can make the films they want to make and ensure their visions are the ones that make it to the screen.
www.hp.com/plus_sundance

sundance institute + hp

= everything is possible

©2003 Hewlett-Packard Company.

hp: Where the Director's Cut is the only Cut
A small fraction of prospective customers will read the product's descriptions in an advertisement. No matter, it's always about the brand. So the idea here is to name names. The copy explains the relationship: hp (or Hewlett Packard) is a partner of a forward-looking company. The invitation to the reader couldn't be clearer: be a part of the equation.

Creative Directors	Steve Luker, Steve Simpson
Associate Creative Director	John Norman
Copywriter	Steve Simpson
Art Director	Hunter Hindman
Photographer	Nitin Vadukul
Art Buyer/Print Producer	Margaret Brett-Kearns
Agency	Goodby, Silverstein & Partners
Client	Hewlitt Packard (hp)

join **us**

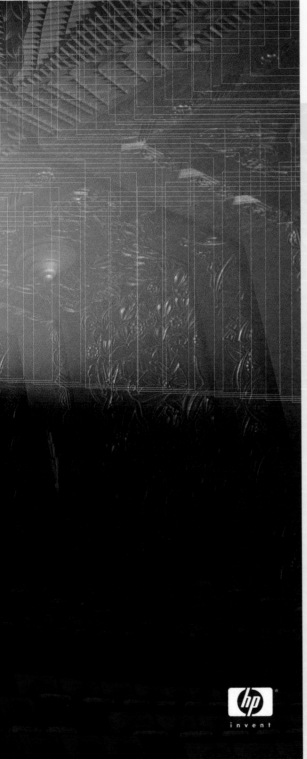

It is widely believed that the combination of legislation, shared design, similar manufacturing techniques, and universal packaging have eliminated meaningful brand differences. Even so, copywriters' tasks have not changed. They are still expected to find words which convince consumers to buy their client's products.

An increasingly popular solution to the dilemma:
Persuade potential consumers that the purchase of a certain product will confirm their membership in an exclusive 'club'.

The 'club' approach is not so much a sales tool as it is an invitation.
1. 'Club' can have literal and figurative connotations.
2. Function is secondary to belonging in the most conspicuous 'club' advertisements targeted to a young audience.
3. Not limited to youth. Today's most prestigious brands are now being positioned to imply 'exclusive' rather than 'exclusion'.

Samsung uses the slogan 'Everyone's Invited'. The proposal intends to appeal to a state of mind. This approach is different from self-image-reinforcement advertising. An invitation advertisement says, 'You won't be simply hip. Your world will be hip.'

Call on the 'club' concept to mean 'exclusive' rather than 'exclusion'.

'Club' can have a literal or figurative meaning.

Don't let governmental regulations get in the way. Go with them.

An advertisement is always about the brand.

A right rule for a club would be, admit no man whose presence excludes any one topic. It requires people who are not surprised and shocked, who do and let do, and let be, who sink trifles, and know solid values, and who take a great deal for granted.

Ralph Waldo Emerson (1803-1882), U.S. essayist, poet, and philosopher, in 'Clubs', Society and Solitude, Boston: Houghton, Mifflin & Co., 1870

With no mind, blossoms invite the butterfly.
With no mind, the butterfly visits the blossom.

One Robe, One Bowl: The Zen Poetry of Ryokan, New York:
Weatherhill, 1977

work
room

There's space for you
at New York's ultimate health club, The Sports Center.

Chelsea Piers, Pier 60, 23rd Street and the Hudson River.

Call 212.336.6000 to join.

Chelsea Piers Sports Center: There's Space for You campaign
When you start to write, think beyond what's obvious. The gymnasium
at New York City's Chelsea Piers Sports Center is about more than the
body. It's also a place to renew the mind and soul. In a city crowded
with packed health clubs, the appeal of a personal space can't be
exaggerated. So this copy invites the reader in with 'There's Space
for You'.

Creative Director   Mark Trippetti
Copywriter   Norm Magnusson
Art Director   Liza Giorsetti
Agency   TURF
Client   Chelsea Piers Sports Center

SHARP.   Liquid crystal television **AQUOS**™

be spirited

©2001 Sharp Corporation

Introducing Aquos, inspiring flat-panel, liquid crystal television. Crystal-clear image quality. Outstanding brightness. And a screen that's merely 2.5 inches thin. Aquos by Sharp. It's what TV will be. sharp-usa.com

be sharp™

Sharp: Be Spirited
Is a new television being advertised? Or is the ad inviting you to stop comparing, thinking, discussing, and simply be? This is a lovely way of saying, 'Buy'. But what you're buying transcends the product. Don't be fooled by the children; it's written for enlightened adults – men and women who want to live in the simple, clean, and happy world of Sharp.

Copywriter   Paul Bernasconi
Art Director   Damian Totman
Agency   Oasis Advertising
Client   Sharp Electronics

About his agency's advertisement for the Volkswagen 'Drivers Wanted' campaign:
Our audience knows who they are. We do, too. We created a club for people who do not normally want to join a club.

Ron Lawner, Executive Creative Director, Arnold Worldwide, in *Creativity* magazine, May 2003

Advertising is selling Twinkies to adults.

Donald R. Vance, American Scholar, about a sweet, chocolate-coated pastry for children, produced by Continental Bakery, Natik, Mass., U.S.

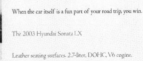

America's Best Warranty
10-Year/100,000-Mile Powertrain Protection
5-Year/60,000-Mile Bumper-to-Bumper Coverage
5-Year/Unlimited Miles 24-hr. Roadside Assistance

HYUNDAI
Win

When beef jerky is breakfast

When the road opens wide

And snake farms get visited

When the view out the window is better than any TV show

And there's room enough to grow closer

When the car itself is a fun part of your road trip, you win.

The 2003 Hyundai Sonata LX

Leather seating surfaces. 2.7-liter, DOHC, V6 engine.

Dual front and front side-impact airbags.

America's Best Warranty.™ All standard.

$19,074¹

[hyundaiUSA.com]

Hyundai: 'Road Trip' The 2003 Hyunda Sonata LX
'Road Trip' isn't an orignal idea but it's a classic. Here it's also a point of departure. Road trips are hard on cars, a fact seldom mentioned. So the text talks about the warranty, too. In this way, it tells the reader that this isn't about one great trip but about many years on the road – together.

Copywriter	David Canright
Art Director	Lynda Hodge
Photographer	Florian Geiss
Print Production	Pam Zmud
Agency	The Richards Group
Client	Hyundai Motor America

serious play

Selling is serious business...however.

Advertising agencies expect the work of the copywriter to drive consumers to the showroom, the supermarket, the mall, the toll-free telephone-ordering number, or the website. But there's little urgency for prospective consumers to buy. There is no shortage of product or purveyors of goods. And, in many cases, no real reason to go shopping.

Even so, copywriters still have to make cash registers ring. As one of these writers, you will hear a great deal about cutting through the clutter.

How to keep the reader's attention:
1. Be nonchalant about the product.
2. Risk telling a joke.
3. Ignore convention.
4. Give a benefit.
5. Don't be obvious.
6. Tease the reader.
7. Seduce the reader.

Serious play requires:
1. Respect for the reader's intelligence.
2. Risk taking.
3. Provocation.
4. A sense of humour.
5. Comfort with self-deprecation.

zipcar: 350 Hours/Year Having Sex...
How many times have your heard, 'Sex sells'? However, it's only true if you're selling sex. What's clever here is how quickly the writer moves from the joke to the brand and promise, although, a reader may linger on the headline for some time. The concept here is relatively new; yet it only takes a moment to learn how to use it.

Creative Director	Martha Shaw
Art Director	Jon Pietz
Account Executive	Nancy Rosenzweig
Production	Jonathan Dupuis
Agency	eFlicks Media
Contact	eFlicksMedia.com
Client	Zipcar

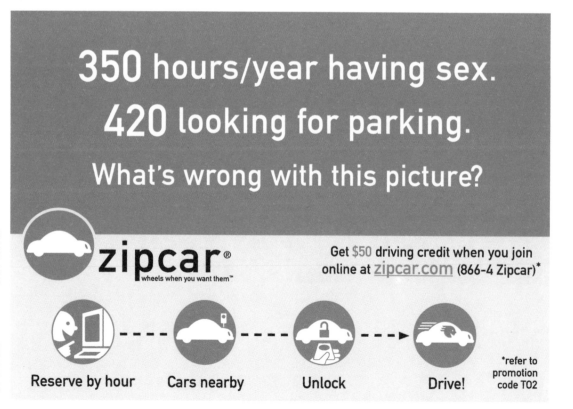

BLUE FROM AMERICAN EXPRESS®
PAY OVER TIME I FREE REWARDS PROGRAM I NO ANNUAL FEE

FORWARD ►

OTHER
CARDS ARE
SO OPAQUE.

CALL 1 800 600 BLUE

<u>American Express: Other Cards Are so Opaque</u>
Often it's what you don't say that's the most persuasive. When the product's benefits aren't particularly compelling, find another way to connect to the reader. Here, the joke at a competing product's expense is made for more than a laugh. It insinuates very clearly: 'We know what's important to you; the others haven't a chance with you.' If customers get the pun, they'll probably want the card.

Creative Director	Fred Lind	
Copywriter	Brad Mislow	
Art Director	Julie Eyerman	
Agency	Ogilvy & Mather	
Client	American Express	

There used to be rules…
and they were easy to
follow.

'Serious' and 'play' are
not necessarily antonyms.

Hang loose.

Play at risk.

I want to stay as close to the edge as I can without going over. Out on the edge, you see all kinds of things you can't see from the center.

Kurt Vonnegut, *Piano Player*, New York: Charles Scribner's Sons, 1952

Lexus: Über Auto
You don't have to compete on the same terms as the competition. Instead, play with the rules, as Lexus does with this mock magazine. This four-page insert doesn't list performance specifications; it doesn't ask the reader to compare and contrast. Rather, it calls on blatant 'misinformation' and introduces the car in an entirely novel way. Its parody of time-honoured conventions makes the claims all the more persuasive.

Chief Creative	James Dalthorp
Copywriter	Craig Crawford
Art Director	James Hendry
Traffic	Tracy Antonio, Brenda Cooksey
Studio Artist	Todd Roberson
Print Producer	Lisa Huber
Account Executive	Shayne Globerson
Photographer	R. J. Muna
Agency	Team One Advertising
Client	Lexus

Willkommen Zu Der Wunderbar Wagen.

Stuttgart nach Munich in der neu Lexus RX 330:
218 kilometers that will forever change the world
of automotive luxury. — Mãtthias Muench

31

Listen, little Elia: draw your chair up close to the edge of the precipice and I'll tell you a story.

F. Scott Fitzgerald (1896–1940), American author, *The Crack-Up*, 'Notebook N', ed. Edmund Wilson (1945)

Harley Earl was here.

Expressive styling is just one of the many legacies of America's greatest car designer.

All of which live on today at the car company where he hung his hat.

BUICK®

THE SPIRIT OF AMERICAN STYLE®

The new 2003 Park Avenue® Ultra at buick.com. ©2002 GM Corp. All rights reserved.

Buick: Harley Earl Was Here
Conjure a ghost. Put a little-known name in the headline. And toss your hat into the ring at a time when fedoras are out of fashion. All this is definitely a risk. But, if you believe your product will meet the challenge, then take the leap. If you think people will be intrigued and want a closer look, go for it. Sometimes you have to trust your instincts. Incidentally, Harley Earl, the 'Da Vinci of Detroit', was the legendary General Motor's designer from the 1920s, up to and including the exuberant Cadillacs of the 1950s.

Executive Creative Director	David Moore
Creative Director	Mike Joiner
Sr Art Director	John Beattie
Advertising &	
Promotions Manager	Michael Hand
Agency	McCann-Erickson Detroit
Client	Buick Motor Division

Permission granted by Michael Hand, Advertising & Promotions Manager, Buick Motor Division.

RBS/Royal Bank of Scotland: Less Talk
No one has ever claimed that financial-service companies must tell their stories with a straight face. But, if there's nothing funny about money, why do amusing financial advertisements work? It's because they reject conventional generic promises and, rather, tell prospective customers exactly what they want to hear.

Ex Creative Director/Copywriter — Simon Dicketts
Art Director — Fergus Flemming
Type Designers — Rob Wilson, Simon Warden
Photographer — Andy Green
Agency — M&C Saatchi
Client — Royal Bank of Scotland

To play is nothing but the imitative substitution of a pleasurable, superfluous and voluntary action for a serious, necessary, imperative and difficult one.

Max J. Friedländer (1867–1958), German art historian, *On Art and Connoisseurship*, London: Bruno Cassirer, 1942, chapt. 3

Raffles Class

Singapore Airlines presents

S P A C E B E D™

The biggest bed in Business Class.

Experience the comfort of the most spacious business class bed in the sky. Raffles Class SpaceBed offers you a new level of luxury with more room to work, relax or sleep. All, of course, while enjoying the inflight service even other airlines talk about.

Best International Airline
Condé Nast Traveler Readers Choice Award
Winner for 14 out of 15 years

SpaceBed to be installed on all flights from North America by June, 2003.

For information, fares and bookings please visit www.sia-spacebed.com

A great way to fly
SINGAPORE AIRLINES

A STAR ALLIANCE MEMBER

Singapore Airlines: SpaceBed
The woman here isn't merely travelling; she's being transported. Had the copy just promised greater comfort, the claim would be both unexceptional and open to debate. But the notion of 'SpaceBed' suggests an entirely different experience of flight.

Creative Director	Gary Caulfield
Senior Art Director	Paul Tilley
Group Account Director	Digby Richards
Account Director	Angelique Tan
Project Manager	Basir Salleh
Worldwide Agency of Record	Batey Pte. Ltd., Singapore
U.S. Agency of Record	Hamon & Associates, Los Angeles
Client	Singapore Airlines

hyperbole and the **art** of the stretch

Hyperbole is an exaggerated or extravagant statement.

While it isn't intended literally, it will enable you nonetheless to make a point. And, because it is more fanciful than fictitious, the use of hyperbole is an effective way to get beneath a person's resistance. What's more, people tend to enjoy it.

Hyperbole allows you to stretch your message without having to hit your reader over the head with it. You can make extravagant claims without challenge because a reasonable person understands you're not really promising the moon. Another advantage: Hyperbole eliminates the need for superlatives or extraneous adjectives.

Hyperbole lets you make big promises in a soft voice.

Hyperbole can speak softly.

Hyperbole can be oblique.

Hyperbole can make unchallenged declarations.

Hyperbole can be amusing.

Everyone speaks in hyperbole.

The variety of circumstances in which style has become the preponderant form of publicly accessible information is endless.

Stuart Ewen, *All Consuming Images: The Politics of Style in Contemporary Culture*, Basic Books, Conclusion, p. 261

Tell all the truth but tell it slant.
Success in circuit lies.

Emily Dickinson (1830-1886), American poet, in Thomas H. Johnson (ed.), *The Complete Poems of Emily Dickinson*, Boston: Little, Brown & Co., 1960

Experience the comf
spacious business cla

WHOOSH

**The world's fastest workgroup color printer has arrived.
The Xerox Phaser® 7300. You'd better hang on.**

There's a new way to look at it.

Now color speeds through any office at 30 ppm. The Xerox Phaser® 7300 tabloid color printer beats all speed records for workgroup color printing.* And at 37 ppm black and white, it eliminates the need for multiple printers. You get consistent 2400-dpi color that's always bright, sharp and brilliant. The Phaser 7300

automatically selects the correct paper size for any job, up to 12 x 18. So experience a colorful flurry of productivity with the Phaser 7300. Or let your office soar with our full line of reliable, award-winning network printers by calling 1-800-362-6567 ext. 1910 or visiting xerox.com/officeprinting/bird1910

THE DOCUMENT COMPANY
XEROX.

Xerox: Whoosh
Why say 'Fast', when you can say 'Whoosh'? The copywriter enjoyed writing it, and the reader enjoys reading it. The use of onomatopoeia, a word to imitate a sound, is one way to dramatise facts you want to share. In technology, speed is the price of entry. Even though it's not particularly exciting, it's nevertheless always relevant. But 'Whoosh' has no limits (see also page 139).

Worldwide Ex Creative Director	Barry Hoffman
Assoc Creative Director/Copywriter	Mike Macina
Senior Art Director	Greg Elkin
Photographer	Robert Ammirati
Agency	Young & Rubicam Advertising
Client	Xerox Corporation

nobody, not even the rain, has such small hands.

e.e. cummings (1894–1962), George J. Firmage (ed.), *Complete Poems, 1904–1962: e.e. cummings*, New York: Liveright; London : W.W. Norton, 1991

Exaggeration! Was ever any virtue attributed to a man without exaggeration? Was ever any vice, without infinite exaggeration? Do we not exaggerate ourselves to ourselves, or do we recognize ourselves for the actual men we are? Are we not all great men? Yet what are we actually, to speak of? We live by exaggeration.

Henry David Thoreau (1817-1862), American philosopher, author, naturalist, 'Thomas Carlyle and His Works' (1847), in *The Writings of Henry David Thoreau*, Boston: Houghton Mifflin Company, 1906, vol. 4, pp. 352-353

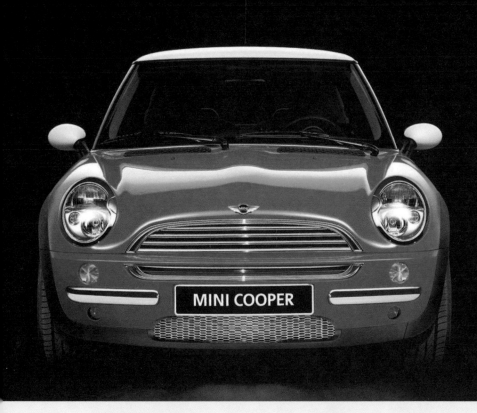

LET'S BURN THE MAPS. Let's get lost. Let's turn right when we should turn left. Let's read fewer car ads and more travel ads. Let's not be back in ten minutes. Let's hold out until the next rest stop. Let's eat when hungry. Let's drink when thirsty. Let's break routines, but not make a routine of it. **LET'S MOTOR.**™

Mini Cooper: Let's Burn the Maps

This advertisement is more than an advertisement. It's a manifesto. It doesn't describe a life but a philosophy of life. And it's not simply news; it's an invitation. When the brand is unique, the copy can take more liberties. The key is consistency. As a copywriter, once you find your road, stay on it.

Creative Director	Alex Bogusky
Associate Creative Director	Andrew Keller
Copywriters	Ari Merkin, Steve O'Connell
Art Director	Mark Taylor
Photographer	Daniel Hartz
Agency	Crispin Porter + Bogusky
	(Creative Dept Coordinator Veronica Padilla)
Client	Mini

Can the design of your workplace help good ideas get out the door?

In today's economy, innovation is key to survival. So where do good ideas come from? Research shows that 80% of all innovations are the direct result of communication—simply talking to one another. Unfortunately, most workplaces don't help support this kind of informal communication. A Pathways environment does. Unlike conventional office furniture, Pathways is a complete portfolio, including everything from walls and flooring to furniture to power, cabling and other technology tools. All are designed around our in-depth understanding of how people work, both alone and together. Paired with thoughtful planning, a Pathways environment can help you better communicate and innovate. In fact, it can free your entire organization to work more effectively. To learn more, click on Pathways at www.steelcase.com.

Steelcase Do what you do better.™

A single idea can change the whole world. But first it must survive the gauntlet of the office. In a Pathways® work

An idea doesn't know where it was born. It knows only that it *is*, and it must not sit still.

place, barriers are eliminated and replaced with conduits: for better thinking, better communication, better work.

Call 800.333.9939 or visit www.steelcase.com.
©2003 Steelcase Inc.
02-0003544

Steelcase Do what you do better.™

Steelcase: An Idea Doesn't Know...
Furniture as a facilitator – as an incubator, as a liberator in the workplace. Even though this company makes desks, chairs and partitions, this advertisement is selling collaboration, creativity, and productivity. Is it a stretch? Yes, but it's an approach that car makers, computer companies, and jeans designers have taken for years.

Agency   Martin Williams
Client   Steelcase, Inc.

Courtesy, Steelcase Inc.

People read copy. They even read bad copy.

Ray Werner, Former Creative Director, Ketchum, later President and Co-Creative Director, Werner Chepelsky & Partners, and then General Manager, Bozell, Pittsburgh, told to Robert Sawyer

Exaggeration is in the course of things. Nature sends no creature, no man into the world, without adding a small excess of his proper quality.

Ralph Waldo Emerson (1803–1882), American essayist, poet, philosopher, 'Nature', *Essays: Second Series*, Boston: J. Munroe and Co., 1844

WHEN THE ASTEROID HITS
AND CIVILIZATION CRUMBLES,
YOU'LL BE READY.

THE NEW H2. **HUMMER** LIKE NOTHING ELSE.   HUMMER.COM

HUMMER: When the Asteroid Hits…
The copy here doesn't make any sense. Well, maybe it makes perfect sense. In fact, the bigger the obstacle and the greater the threat, the truer the message is. How far can you take hyperbole? As far as you dare, providing you stay true to or in character with the brand.

Creative Directors	Lance Jensen, Gary Koepke
Art Director	Will Uronis
Copywriter	Shane Hutton
Photography	Tim Simmons
Agency	Modernista!
Client	HUMMER (Div GM)

2003 General Motors Corporation.
Used with permission of HUMMER and General Motors.

Sony: Fresh
Greater fidelity and sharper, clearer sound is old news. But 'fresh' music, this is unique. Whether or not it means anything is beside the point. It's not really intended to mean anything. The copy is written to help the prospective customer imagine that this new technology offers incredible sound. It's believable because it's unbelievable.

Copywriter	Corey Rakowsky
Art Director	Kleber Menezes
Photography	2A Photography
Agency	Young & Rubicam
Client	Sony

Once you drive one, there's no turning back.

Ahh, marriage. An agreement to spend your lives together. So what's another hour or two apart? Especially when spent in the E 500 Sedan with its 5-liter V-8 engine. Hey, Mr. Right will understand that the allure is almost impossible to resist. Call 1-800-FOR-MERCEDES or visit us at MBUSA.com. **The E-Class. Experience. Unlike any other.**

Mercedes-Benz: 'Wedding'
<u>Once You Drive One, There's No Turning Back</u>
When you're truly provocative your reader's response will be involuntary. The cliché, 'Left at the Altar', is made new because it's the groom who's being abandoned. It's a very modern idea because the word 'agreement' in the text to define marriage also says the times have changed. It's all tongue-in-cheek, but there's truth in jest (see also pages 16–17 and 58).

Creative Director	Andy Hirsch
Copywriter	Jeff Vinick
Art Director	Mike Rosen
Photography	Wedding scene courtesy of Corbis/Car by Tim Damon
Agency	Merkley + Partners New York
Client	Mercedes-Benz

Courtesy of Mercedes-Benz USA.

Great brands never compromise who they are, so it was a matter of saying [in one of our advertisements], 'This is who I am, how I am. You're either with me or you're not.'

Cindy Gallop, Bartle Bogle Hegarty advertising agency, New York City, in *Print* magazine, no. LVII, 2003

provocation

It's easy to be provocative.

It's also easy to step outside of what's generally considered socially acceptable. Someone will always be excited or offended by something.

Provocative advertisements usually have some overt sexual or political content, such as the Calvin Klein or Benetton campaigns. But, then, there are those that are rude and vulgar or touch on the taboo, an approach often justified by a claimed necessity to stand out. But an advertisement which merely provokes anger or embarrassed laughter will rarely increase brand awareness and seldom motivates a consumer to buy.

Provocation can also be subtle. Knowledge of the audience includes an awareness of what will prompt a favourable response. Sometimes no more than a fresh twist on an old idea is required. Or a *double entendre* can be used, one so easy to miss that a reader will wonder if it's intentional. In fact, if you want to reflect on what's sincerely provocative, then 'Think Small' as copywriter Bill Bernbach suggested concerning the Volkswagen Beetle or just 'Think Different' about Apple.

WRITING COPY

Samsung: DigitAll Temptation
Some words automatically provoke a reaction. When people read them, their minds will probably go in a predictable direction. In this headline, the neologism 'DigitAll' – a play on 'digital' – is paired with 'temptation'. The promise described in the copy is 'this state-of-the-art TV will entrance you'. But the headline has already prepared the reader to fall in love.

Creative Director/Copywriter — Luke Bailey
Creative Director /Art Director — Jim Mochnsky
Agency — Foote, Cone and Belding Worldwide, New York
Client — Samsung Electronics

Courtesy Samsung Electronics America, Inc. reprinted by permission.

Your audience gives you everything you need. They tell you. There is no director who can direct you like an audience.

Fanny Brice (1891-1951), American entertainer, in Norman Katkov, *The Fabulous Fanny*, New York: Alfred A. Knopf, 1952, chapt. 6

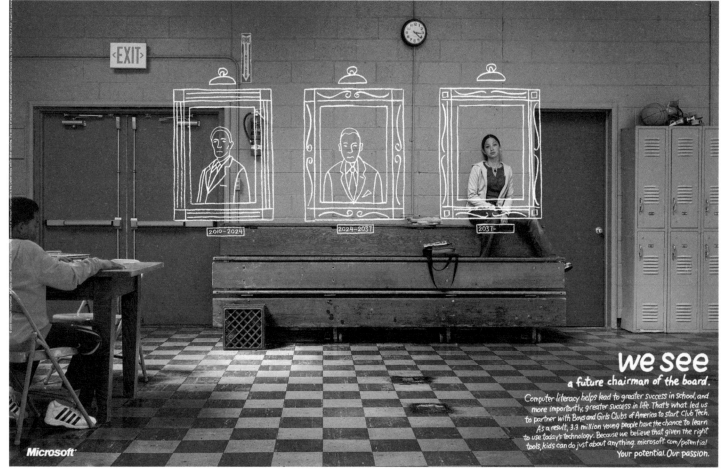

Microsoft Corporate: 'Boys and Girls Club'
Obviously, provocation is a device to get the reader's attention. But in this advertisement, the writer didn't have to shout to provoke. Most people still think of the chairman of the board as, well, a man. When you challenge this expectation – say, put a woman at the head of the table – you'll unleash strong emotions in the reader.

Ex Creative Director/Copywriter   Dante Lombardi
Ex Creative Director/ Art Directors Walt Connelly, Ashley Reese
Photographer   Kiran Masters
Agency   McCann-Erickson SF
Client   Microsoft (Contact: Peter Cohen)

ABSOLUT SANCTITY.

A DILEMMA FOR THE GLASSBLOWER: How does one rinse the bottle that is to hold such a pristine spirit? THE SOLUTION: Rinse with ABSOLUT. Then fill with ABSOLUT.

OUR DEVOTION TO PERFECTION IS ABSOLUT.

Absolut: Absolut Sanctity
Few approaches are as provocative as blurring the lines between the sacred and the profane. Here Absolut is no longer merely punning, but using words such as 'sanctity', 'spirit' and 'devotion' for their unmistakably religious significance. It's not difficult to read the word absolution in this context. Is this ad asking the reader to keep the faith?

Creative Director	Joseph Mazzaferro
Art Director	Andy Hall
Agency	TBWA/Chiat/Day New York
Client	Absolut

I am sorry to think that you do not get a man's most effective criticism until you provoke him. Severe truth is expressed with some bitterness.

Henry David Thoreau (1817–1862), American philosopher, author, naturalist. B. Torrey and F. H. Allen (eds.), *Journals*, 14 vols., 1906, entry for March 15, 1854

human **face**

Abstract ideas are difficult to follow.

Products and services blend into one another. Promises come and go. At the same time, people expect information in smaller and smaller bites. So how will you tell your story? One way is to write to a human face.

Whether the depiction is straightforward, idealised, or treated with humour, this form is different from the familiar, and often mocked, 'every mom', found in slice-of-life advertising. In that approach, a particular face is used to encourage the reader to think: 'I'm like this woman'. Or, 'I aspire to her life; therefore this product is perfect for me.'

Here, the reader is not asked to identify with the face in the ad, but to associate the qualities of that person with the brand. For example, strong silent type translates into reliable, honest brand. Your copy will have to tell complex stories in fast, simple prose. But as part of a creative team, you'll also be asked to consider what type of face will best illuminate the values communicated by your copy.

A face has the ability to:
1. Serve as an archetype.
2. Ground an abstract concept.
3. Help tell a story.
4. Evoke humour.
5. Inform and inspire.

A face can create intimate connections.

A face can make the unreal real.

The face of a person can be the face of a brand.

Except in beauty advertisements, a beautiful face is not required.

Celebrities, though they shine above us, are also very much like us. The whole story of their success is that they came from 'the mass'.

Stuart Ewen, *All Consuming Images: The Politics of Style in Contemporary Culture*, New York: Basic Books Chapter 5, P. 94

It is safe to say that Mr. Green and his Fujifilm FinePix S602 Zoom Digital Camera are firmly planted in their 'green period.' With 3.1 million pixels, a 3rd Generation Super CCD and the versatility of both auto and manual focus, Mr. Green sacrifices nothing in creativity. Add to that a 6x Zoom and the ability to work in continuous shooting mode and it's easy to see why the FinePix S602 is the perfect partner for anyone who has the eye of a photographer. For some, it's sunsets. For others, it's grass. For information call 1-800-800-FUJI or go to fujifilm.com.

GET THE PICTURE

MR. GREEN GETS HOOKED ON GRASS.

©2002 Fuji Photo Film U.S.A., Inc.

 FUJIFILM

Fujifilm: Mr. Green Gets Hooked on Grass
The enthusiast, the gifted amateur, is another archetype. But this advertisement isn't an endorsement. It's for a company better known for making photo film, not for a digital camera. And there is no Mr Green. Here the writer makes an interesting choice – he puts Mr Green in the copy perhaps because the face is partially obscured or because the agency people couldn't decide on what type of face would best portray this brand's values.

Copywriter	Mark Bernath
Art Director	Tom Godici
Photographer	Jake Chessum
Agency	Publicis
Client	Fujifilm

Where to find a 200-year-old company.

DUPONT 200 YEARS

You don't get to be a 200-year-old company by keeping up with the times. You do it by staying ahead of them. With discoveries like LYCRA®, the DuPont stretch fiber that revolutionized swimwear, with remarkable fit and freedom of movement. At DuPont, we're proud to begin our third century of innovation in everything from jets to jeans to crops to countertops.

The miracles of science®

www.dupont.com or 1-800-441-7515

DuPont: Where to Find a 200-Year-Old Company
Women are ascendant today – women athletes in particular. They're also hard for the eye to resist. This advertisement celebrates a company's remarkable longevity. However, it isn't a history lesson. It invites the reader to share a future. The copy says it – but so does the face. This woman knows where she's going and isn't looking back; neither is the company.

Creative Directors	Katie Peabody, Peter Barba
U.S. DuPont Brand Manager	Barbara Pandos
Agency	McCann-Erickson New York
Client	DuPont

Human models are more vivid and more persuasive than explicit moral commands.

Daniel J. Boorstin (1914–2004), American historian, Pulitzer-prize winning author, and the Librarian of Congress from 1975 to 1987

123

The reasonable man adapts himself to the world; the unreasonable one persists in trying to adapt the world to himself. Therefore, all progress depends on the unreasonable man.

George Bernard Shaw (1856-1950), Anglo-Irish playwright, 'Maxims for Revolutionists: Reason', *Man and Superman: A Comedy and a Philosophy*, London: A. Constable, 1903

ITT Industries irrigates
over 10,000,000 acres of land in the U.S.
Meanwhile, Ben Paulsen has 150 acres
of wheat to harvest.

From Maine to Hawaii, our Goulds pumps bring water to almost 16,000 square miles of land. Hidden, submerged or even buried, these mechanical hearts fill the lifelines to over 10,000,000 acres day in and day out.

ITT believes technology should be invisible. People don't have to think a lot about our engineering. Its benefits, on the other hand, cover the landscape.

FLUID TECHNOLOGY · Goulds Pumps · Lowara
DEFENSE ELECTRONICS AND SERVICES
ELECTRONIC COMPONENTS
MOTION AND FLOW CONTROL

ITT Industries
Engineered for life

www.itt.com

ITT Industries: ITT Industries Irrigates...
Certain faces are symbolic. The family farmer isn't the audience for this ad. He's here because in the pantheon of American heroes, this endangered species stands tall. But the copy never refers to the man in the truck. It tells the story the company wants to tell. But readers will feel good about the brand because they believe in what the farmer represents.

Creative Director	Danny Gregory
Copywriter	Phil Kann
Art Director	Guy Marino
Photographer	Doug Menuez
Agency	Doremus
Client	ITT Industries

Advertisers are the interpreters of our dreams...

E.G. White, American author and editor, in Robert Andrews,
The Columbia Dictionary of Quotations, New York: Columbia
University Press, 1993, p. 19

You now have to decide what 'image' you want for your brand. Image means personality. Products, like people, have personalities, and they can make or break them in the market place.

David Ogilvy, *Ogilvy on Advertising*, New York: Vintage Books, 1985, p. 14

MetLIfe: Dreams are for Passing on...
One type of face is caricature. It uses humour to capture a reader's
attention and weaken resistance. This headline sounds like something
this man might say. But the advertisement isn't about the butcher.
Except as an idea, he doesn't exist. In fact, the job of the copy is to
describe the product so that the reader feels an advertisement was
written for him or her.

Copywriter	Betsy Petropoulos
Art Director	Cynthia Herrli
Art Buyer	Grier Hynes
Print Producer	Vic Ferrarelli
Account Management	Gerald Siano
Agency	Young & Rubicam NY
Client	MetLife

Reprinted with permission from Metropolitan Life Insurance Company, 2003.
PEANUTS © United Feature Syndicate, Inc.

talk the **talk**

Copy can sound strangely impersonal if it attempts to avoid alienating someone, somewhere. When writers try to circumvent regulations and avoid challenges, they often fall back on generic descriptions, empty promises, and generalities. So why is it surprising when someone, particularly a client, says, 'No one reads copy anymore'?

As consumers grow more sophisticated, they also become more discriminating. Therefore, it's increasingly more difficult to sell something to them, unless that something is right for them.

Because consumers' free time has diminished and discretionary income has increased, they're only interested in learning about products or services that will, as marketers say, 'impact on their lives'. This belief has germinated the 'consumer as hero' and relegated the product to a supporting role.

So how do you write to these new consumers, intent on being the 'stars of their own movies'? You talk the talk.

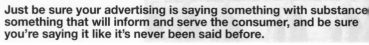

Just be sure your advertising is saying something with substance, something that will inform and serve the consumer, and be sure you're saying it like it's never been said before.

William 'Bill' Bernbach, advertising pioneer, *Bill Bernbach Said…*, New York: DDB Needham Worldwide, 1989

Talk about what's relevant.

Know all about the potential customer.

Speak the language of your audience.

Are you writing authentic jargon or gibberish?

Strange things happen in 10 feet of visibility.

Twenty-five years at the helm. Over 60,000 hours logged. Thousands of tons of cargo hauled. And there's still nothing you can do when fog rolls in. On top of the damage to the vessel, your fuel tank empties into the surrounding river. Now you're without a ship and responsible for thousands of dollars in cleanup costs.

WQIS marine pollution insurance anticipates what you can't.

Things go wrong, from bad luck to terrible accidents. Which is why more vessel owners and operators choose WQIS for their marine pollution insurance. It's a fact, no one has more experience cleaning up spills, or offers more innovative coverage to the marine community.

Sail with Experience

Have your broker contact WQIS for a quote today.
212-292-8700
www.wqis.com

WQIS

Strange things happen when the channel chart is older than the channel.

The map didn't indicate a pipeline but the brown liquid surfacing around your spud tells you differently. Depending on the size of that pipeline, you could be looking at hundreds of thousands of gallons of oil being emptied into the waterway. The fact you had a map doesn't let you off the hook.

WQIS marine pollution insurance protects you from expensive surprises.

Things go wrong, from bad luck to terrible accidents. Which is why more vessel owners and operators choose WQIS for their marine pollution insurance. It's a fact, no one has more experience cleaning up spills, or offers more innovative coverage to the marine community.

Sail with Experience

Have your broker contact WQIS for a quote today.
212-292-8700
www.wqis.com

WQIS

Strange things happen after a spill is contained.

It was only a small spill. The cleanup shouldn't have been a problem. There was time to make it right, but mistakes were made and things got out of hand. Suddenly a cleanup that should've cost $1000 is now more than five times that. And you did everything you were supposed to.

WQIS coverage and MPRG response insure that once a spill is contained the episode is over.

MPRG is WQIS' action arm in the field. When spills happen, MPRG is there for clients. The first 24 hours of a spill are the most critical. Within hours of notification, MPRG response experts are on the scene executing strategies to maximize the effectiveness of the cleanup and minimize costs.

Sail with Experience

<u>WQIS: Strange Things Happen… campaign</u>
Don't assume that anyone will pay attention to an advertisement you write just because it's in a trade publication, one that has a professional readership in a certain discipline. And don't presume that anyone is listening just because you're talking. The copywriter of this campaign gives the professional a real reason to care and says something both compelling and relevant.

Creative Directors — James Connor, Robert Sawyer
Copywriters — Robert Sawyer, Bryan Jenkins
Art Director — Bryan Jenkins
Photography — Professional Mariner Stock Photography
Agency — The James Group
Client — WQIS

**Manhattan is an island.
You shouldn't be.**

Social Circles has a membership of over 2,200 fun-loving, curious and successful professionals. And we're always looking to add one more. Visit SocialCircles.com to find out about our more than 60 events per month.

S Social Circles® | New York's Premier Activity Club!
www.socialcircles.com

Social Circles: Manhattan is an Island
Urban Outings: You're out of the Closet/More Meet, Less Market
The more specialised a market is, the more nuances there are. And the smaller the customer niche is, the more protective is the marketplace of its members. So don't try to fake it or to write from the outside looking in. The key here is authenticity. Social Circles reaches out to heterosexuals, and Urban Outing, to homosexual men. (The two organisations, while they appear to be entirely different, are part of the Connect Marketing and Entertainment Group.)

Copywriters   Jose de Lasa, Brian Stein
Art Director   Adi Ben Hur
Agency   In house
Clients   Social Circles/Urban Outings

Social Circles and Urban Outings are trademarked properties or brands of the Connect
Marketing & Entertainment Group.network of properties.

Brands are built by individuals who have a passion for their craft, and an uncontrollable urge to learn – be it from a research study or a dinner, from a strategy statement or a song.

Dan Wieden of Wieden + Kennedy, in *one. a magazine* published by The One Club for Art and Copy, vol. 6, no. 2, theme 'think small', fall 2002

Are you talkin' to me? Are you talkin' to me?

Robert De Niro as Travis Bickle in Martin Scorsese's (dir.) and Paul Schrader's (writer),
Taxi Driver, Columbia Pictures, 1976

Jargon is the verbal sleight of hand that makes the old hat seem newly fashionable; it gives an air of novelty and specious profundity to ideas that, if stated directly, would seem superficial, stale, frivolous, or false. The line between serious and spurious scholarship is an easy one to blur, with jargon on your side.

David Lehman, 'Archie Debunking', *Signs of the Times: Deconstruction and the Fall of Paul de Man*, New York: Poseidon Press, 1991, chapt. 3

Beautiful business. Ugly practices.

There is an ugly underside to the fashion business. There's waste. Inefficiency. And a tendency to repeat costly errors.

Roundhouse has the solution. EDI processing. Best practices consulting. IT support. All created exclusively for the apparel and consumer products industry.

To raise your Order Fulfillment Rate, lower your Return Rate, increase Shipping Speed and do beautiful business, **Call Tony Lu at 212-244-8081.**

Schedule a Roundhouse Assessment and Action Plan. Call today and **save $1,000*.**

*A Roundhouse Assessment and Action Plan costs $3,000. But schedule one by October 1st, and we will take $1,000 off the price.

roundhouse
we know the business.™

www.roundhousegroup.com

Roundhouse: The Business campaign
Don't give the reader what they want. Give them what they need. To know the difference, do your homework. You must know not only all about the product, but also all about the industry. Learn the language, meet the players and, most important, find the solution.

Creative Director/Copywriter	Robert Sawyer
Art Director	Bryan Jenkins
Photograph	Getty Images
Agency	The James Group
Client	Roundhouse

gobble.

looking for the place to indulge your appetite for a good bargain?

Krups "Duothek" dual coffee maker. 10-cup carafes, two independent brewing systems for reg. or decaf, **your call**. optional infusion basket for tea. black or white. reg. $169.99 sale $149.99

Edgecraft Chef's Choice® Diamond Hone® knife sharpener. 2-stage, 100% diamond abrasives create razor sharp, double bevel edges. tip to bolster. $59.99 **very cutting edge**

round or oval wire baskets in non-corrosive silverplated finish. round 9.5'd. oval 7.5" x 11" **(yet practical)** each $12.00

from freezer to oven to table, Casa Stone by Casafina. **your casa, my casa, our casa.** coordinated colors. microwave and dishwasher safe. shown: 9-3/4'd pasta/pizza server $20.00, 2-1/2 qt. open casserole $34.00, 15-3/4" oval platter $40.00

whatever your district, our garment rack holds, folds, and stores. commercial weight tubular chrome steel with heavy duty casters. expands 50" to 72" long by 66" high. sale $89.99

16-piece European stemware set, 8 white wine, 8 red wine, gift boxed with handle. sale $24.99 **I'll drink to that**

8 oz. Wine-Away, instant red wine stain remover, $7.99. 8 oz. Weiman Wax Away, candle wax remover, $6.99. 18 oz. Hagerty Silver Foam, for flatware and serving pieces, $9.99. **out darn spot!**

All-Clad roaster set includes bonus oven mitts and rack ($41 value). polished stainless steel. 16" x 13" x 3". total value $301. special purchase $199.99 **they'll be glad you chose All-Clad**

Bron mandoline with slicing and julienne blades. stainless steel construction, stand and fingerguard included. **everyone's favorite** reg. $139 sale $99.99

Porto-Top 48" table extender. enables 8 to sit at table for 4. black vinyl over hardboard. sale $39.99 **who has 8 friends?**

warming trays as sleek **as the Museum of Modern Art** selected for its contemporary style. easy to clean, adjustable thermostat, and hot spot 40° warmer than surrounding surface. by Maxim. 21" x 11-3/4" sale $54.99, 28" x 12-3/8" sale $79.99

warm your plate, titillate your palate. our plate warmer warms up to 10 plates right at the dinner table. sale $34.99

from Cuisinart® Stratford 45-piece set. service for eight includes 5-piece hostess set. 18/10 stainless, continental sizing and dishwasher safe. $99 **they'll applaud**

from Towle® Silversmiths: each Copenhagen product features universal pattern, silverplate, green velvet gift box. **give and hope to receive.** ladle, pie server, serving fork, serving spoon each $12.00

All-Clad multi-cooker. 12 qt. stainless steel stock pot, strainer insert and steamer basket. $99.99. **you'll be glad...**

mission style design folding table and chairs. fine furniture details. dark mahogany, premium leather-like black vinyl. 32" sq. table, sale $59.99. chair sale $39.99 **mission possible!**

Look no further.
GRACIOUS HOME®

www.gracioushome.com

phone orders: 212-517-6300 800-338-7809 • fax orders: 212-517-5240 • open 7 days. free delivery in Manhattan. we ship anywhere. gift certificates available.

west broadway at 67th street • 212-231-7800   **east** third ave at 70th street • 212-517-6300

intermediate markdowns may have been taken. prices good through December 10, 2002.

To talk without thinking is to shoot without aiming.

18th-century English proverb

More talk is not as good as less talk, and less talk is not as good as none at all.

Chinese proverb

schmooze.

[4 black padded vinyl chairs, sale $59.99.
34½"sq. x 27½"h matching table, sale $39.99.]

Look no further.®
GRACIOUS HOME®

west broadway at 67th street   212-231-7800
east third avenue at 70th street   212-517-6300
new lighting store 1201 third avenue   212-517-6300
www.gracioushome.com, free delivery in Manhattan. we ship anywhere. sale ends December 10, 2002.

resolve.

[electronic bathroom scale from Measurement Specialties.
permanent lifetime lithium battery, white, 330 lb. capacity,
4 digit readout in .5 lb. increments. sale $29.99]

Look no further.®
GRACIOUS HOME®

east third ave at 70th   212-517-6300
west broadway at 67th   212-231-7800
www.gracioushome.com, free delivery in Manhattan. we ship anywhere. sale ends Jan. 22, 2002.

Gracious Home: Housewares campaign
When using patois, slang, jargon, lingo, or idiom, you must feel them
and be sensitive to them, or they just sound like gibberish. The
successful use of the vernacular depends on three essentials: it's
descriptive; it has relevance, and it feels sincere. ('Schmooze' is Yiddish
for 'chat'.)

Creative Director	Peter Rogers
Art Director	Steffanie Gillstrap
Agency	AGENCYSACKS
Client	Gracious Home

...talk that does not end in any kind of action is better suppressed altogether.

Thomas Carlyle (1795-1881), Scottish writer, Inaugural Address (April 2, 1866),
'Inaugural Address at Edinburgh', *The Harvard Classics*, New York: P.F. Collier &
Son, 1909-14, vol. XXV, part 4

**WORLD LEADERS. ROYAL FAMILIES. POP STARS. THE POPE.
(OUR DEMOGRAPHIC.)**

For over half a century, Land Rovers have been transporting very important people to very important places. Peace summits. Coronations. Sold-out concert venues. And somewhere between Winston Churchill and the Pope, it occurred to us: If we're going to be carrying luminaries, shouldn't we lavish them in absolute comfort and style? And so we created our first Range Rover. Should you be so fortunate as to drive the 2002 4.6 HSE, you'll discover our initial goal has evolved nicely. With advances that include Electronic Air Suspension, a 460-watt, 12-speaker Harman Kardon sound system and leather and burlwood interior appointments, our latest Range Rover stands ready to impress. Precisely the effect it had on the editors of *Kiplinger's*, who rated the Range Rover 4.6 HSE first for safety among SUVs. Now only one question remains: What history will you make in it?

RANGE ROVER

Range Rover: World Leaders...
This advertisement knows what matters to its potential customer —
whose opinions are important to it, with whom they identify, and what
their aspirations are. In your own work, try to know your readers better
than they know themselves.

Copywriter	Cameron Day
Art Director	Lou Flores
Group Creative Directors	David Crawford, Jeremy Postaer
Agency	GSD&M
Client	Land Rover

Why should you trust us during these difficult times?

Because we understand what your investments mean to your family

Investing is an obligation, but it's also a joy.

It's a responsibility we mustn't put off. And, in times like today, it doesn't make sense to wait and see what will happen next. Yes, it's difficult out there, but we believe we can help you, and your family.

What can working with a financial consultant accomplish today? We can help you to protect your equity and to manage risk. And in doing so, we can help you do the best for your family. Managing risk isn't a new approach for us; it is what we do every day for our own families.

What we will do and how we will do it.

Work to protect your equity. Our first job is to protect your equity because it is your money. It's what you have worked so hard to accumulate. It's the difference between comfort and worry. If your investments are not performing to your expectations, lets talk and see what alternatives there are.

Risk management is at the heart of our investment strategy. The better we know the risks, the better we will know how to avoid them. We have many risk management strategies designed to help protect your equity, including technical analysis to discipline our recommendations while removing the emotional attachment to a particular investment. What's more, we know how to respond to the impersonal forces that influence the market. In the end, we will help you to find the right steps to take, because we never forget why you are investing.

Work to Manage the Risk. We don't have to tell you the market is volatile. You've seen it with your own eyes. You've discussed it with your family, your friends, and even your current broker or advisor. You may even have taken steps to protect your portfolio. The question is has any of it really worked to your satisfaction? We can't promise a specific rate of return, but we can promise to do our best to protect your portfolio and increase its value.

What is the true value of your money?

We don't invest to get rich. People invest to help secure the best life for their families, to give their children the best education possible, and to play an important role in their community. But ultimately, people invest to reaffirm their commitment to their families.

If you understand, as we do, the true importance of protecting your money call us today. We promise a high level of professional and personal commitment. We can make this promise because the techniques and strategies we will recommend are the same as those we use to manage and help protect our own family investments.

To us, risk management means seeking growth only after working to protect your investment. To schedule a free portfolio review, please fill out and mail the coupon below. Or to simply talk about your concerns and goals call or email Financial Consultants Steven Hoffman or Michael Seelenfreund at 212.699.7881 or 800.347.4782 shoffman@fahnestock.com, mseelenfreund@fahnestock.com

---

☐ *Yes, I accept your offer for a free portfolio review.*
Please contact me:

Name:

Address:

Phone Number:

Best time to reach you: *please circle:* AM / PM

Steven Hoffman
and
Michael Seelenfreund
Financial Consultants

FAHNESTOCK
E S T A B L I S H E D   1 8 8 1
member NYSE and SIPC

Please mail coupon to: Steven Hoffman, Fahnestock & Co. Inc. • 810 Seventh Avenue New York, NY 10019

Advertising is a valuable economic factor because it is the cheapest way of selling goods, particularly if the goods are worthless.

Sinclair Lewis (1885-1951), American novelist, in *Gideon Planish*, New York: Random House, 1943

money talks

FINALLY,

A MIDSIZE SUV FOR

THE SIDE OF YOU THAT

WANTS EVERYTHING.

THE NEW, WELL-EQUIPPED KIA SORENTO. STARTING UNDER $20,000.

10 YR / 100,000 MILE LIMITED POWERTRAIN WARRANTY

5 YEAR/60,000 MILE LIMITED BASIC WARRANTY
5 YEAR 24-HOUR ROADSIDE ASSISTANCE

For the first time ever, love and logic have come together in one midsize SUV. The all-new Sorento for 2003. It's got everything you could ever want in an SUV. Big, powerful V6 engine. Standard. Dual front and side curtain airbags. Standard. Power windows, mirrors

and locks. Automatic transm... dard. And get this. The Soren... for less than $20,000. To tal...

Price based on MSRP for LX base model excluding taxes, title, license, freight, options and retailer charges. EX model shown costs extra. Actual prices set by retailer. See retailer for warranty details or go to kia.com.

KIA: Finally, A Midsize SUV...
Listing price is common in automobile advertising. Nevertheless, probably no one will admit to having bought a car because it was affordable. The writer of this advertisement knows this, so the copy talks about desire and reason as 'love and logic'. The idea is to help readers reconcile their wants and needs.

Creative Director	Nigel Williams
Copywriter	Kim Genkinger
Art Director	Will Chau
Photographer	R. J. Muna
Agency	davidandgoliath
Client	Kia Motors America

The deeper problems connected with advertising come less from the unscrupulousness of our 'deceivers' than from our pleasure in being deceived, less from the desire to seduce than from the desire to be seduced.

Daniel J. Boorstin (1914-2004), American historian, Pulitzer-prize winning author, and the Librarian of Congress from 1975 to 1987

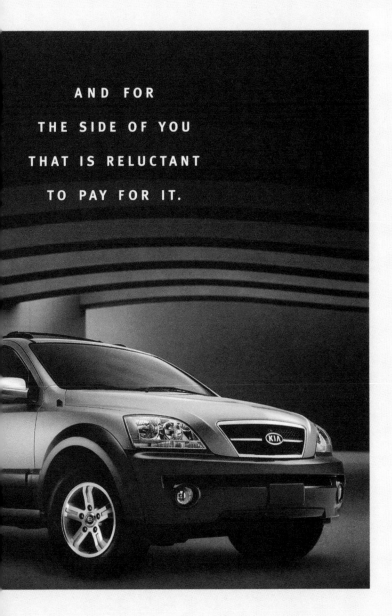

AND FOR

THE SIDE OF YOU

THAT IS RELUCTANT

TO PAY FOR IT.

...CD. And Kia's 10 year/100,000 mile limited powertrain warranty. All stan-

Reasonable. Rational. However you want to say it, you can get into the Sorento

...isit your local Kia retailer or visit kiasorento.com. And bring both sides of you.

KIA
Make every mile count.

People's needs occur and reoccur.

The desires of people are infinite and infinitely evolving. Store shelves are stocked and restocked. Showrooms are filled and refilled. Window displays are built and rebuilt. Sales catalogues appear regularly in the mail. Advertisements are being sent to every address – whether a street address or an email address. Everything, everywhere is for sale. And when it doesn't sell at the list price, it's sold at a discount.

But when money becomes the issue, then price becomes the message. When economic times are hard, cost can't be ignored or hidden as fine print. Price becomes the selling proposition. This is when savings can be put right in the headline, as in 'Up to 50% off'. This is also when code words, such as 'special', 'blowout', and 'promotion' are used. A copywriter can be subtle. But subtle only to a point, because moving the merchandise is everything.

When price is important, you can be clever, but not too subtle.

Remove the preciousness about money.

Rich people like to save money.

Money is a highly emotional issue; people kill for it.

A fool and his money are soon parted.

Traditional aphorism

Don't confuse selling with art.

Jack Taylor, vice-chairman, Jordan McGrath advertising, in Randall Rothenberg, *Where the Suckers Moon: An Advertising Story*, New York: Alfred A. Knopf, 1994

IF THEY BOTH COST THE SAME
WHICH WOULD YOU CHOOSE?

ConnectFirst. A free upgrade from Coach to First Class.
Given the choice, why not move up to First Class space, comfort and amenities for no extra charge?
You can with ConnectFirst from Northwest Airlines. Just buy a full-fare Coach Class ticket with
a connection through Detroit, Minneapolis or Memphis. Some restrictions apply. Book and
buy online at nwa.com, call your travel agent or call Northwest Airlines at 1-800-225-2525.

NORTHWEST AIRLINES.

**To advertise when trade is dull
Is useless, don't you see?
I advertise each day, and trade
Is never dull with me.**

Printers' Ink magazine, January 9,
1895, vol. 12, p. 44

Northwest Airlines: If They Both Cost the Same...
The headline, posed as a question here, has a purpose. It shifts the
discussion from price to other considerations. Retail language in the
copy – such as 'no extra charge' – diverts attention from the actual out-
of-pocket cost to a more abstract idea: flying first class for the cost of
flying in coach.

Creative Director	Markham Cronin
Copywriter	Pete Demarest
Art Director	Dave Schad
Photographer	Craig Perman
Agency	Carmichael Lynch
Client	Northwest Airlines

**You must stir it and stump it,
And blow your own trumpet,
Or trust me, you haven't a chance.**

W.S. Gilbert (1884–1962), toy manufactuer, in Margaret
Miner and Hugh Rawson, *The New International Dictionary of
Quotations*, New York: Penguin Books, 1986 p. 288

A member of
The Leading Hotels of the World

WWW.PENINSULA.COM

Stay IN A WINTER WONDERLAND

INTRODUCING THE WEEKEND PACKAGE AT THE PENINSULA NEW YORK

*Enjoy
special rates of
$350 per night
for a Superior
guestroom.*

Few things are as magical as Manhattan in the winter. And now you can take advantage of the
city's splendor with *The Peninsula New York Weekend Package*. From now until March 31, 2002,
check in on Friday or Saturday and stay for two extraordinary nights, including Continental
breakfast daily and complimentary use of our health club, at a special rate of $350/night.
It's a wonderful way to experience a winter's weekend in Manhattan. *Stay well*

THE PENINSULA
NEW YORK

700 Fifth Avenue at 55th Street   (212) 956-2888   For reservations, please contact your travel professional.
Subject to availability and some restrictions may apply.

HONG KONG   MANILA   BANGKOK   BEIJING   BEVERLY HILLS   CHICAGO

Peninsula: Stay in a Winter Wonderland
Discounts and packages are not glamorous. Even though the affluent
are as eager to save money as anyone is, they don't wish to be known
as wanting to. So here, the copy romances the reader, invites her to
experience something 'wonderful'. As for the low price, it's presented as
a privilege, not a necessity.

Creative Director	Lynn Kokorsky
Copywriter	Beth Levine
Photographer	Doug Menuez
Agency	AGENCYSACKS
Client	Peninsula Hotel Group

EUREKA

We discovered how to bring down the running cost of color for any office to under 10 cents a page. And that was no accident. Introducing the Xerox DocuColor 2240 and 1632 Printer/Copiers. There's a new way to look at it.

Introducing a dazzling breakthrough in color. The Xerox DocuColor® 2240 and 1632 bring the running cost* of making color prints and copies in your office to less than 10 cents a page. And remarkably, reduce black and white running costs to a mere 1.3 cents a page. So for color

and black and white that are easy to use and afford, remember the Xerox DocuColor 2240 and the 1632. Once you discover them, you'll see how simple it can be to integrate color into everything you do. To get all the benefits of low-cost color in your office, get in touch today.

THE DOCUMENT COMPANY
XEROX.

Visit: www.xerox.com/eureka Call: 1-800-ASK-XEROX ext. 2240A

Xerox: Eureka
This exuberant headline literally means, 'I've found it', in ancient Greek. From headline to subhead to copy, readers are told the product will save them money. The tone of the copy is upbeat and positive. The promise is repeated throughout. Cost is the real issue here, and subtlety would be inappropriate (see also page 114).

Worldwide Ex Creative Director	Barry Hoffman
Assoc Creative Director/Copywriter	Mike Macina
Senior Art Director	Greg Elkin
Photographer	Robert Ammirati
Agency	Young & Rubicam Advertising
Client	Xerox Corporation

wordplay

Fast, simple, quick are at the heart of wordplay.

The pun, *double entrendre*, and punchline are some regular forms for playing with words. Sometimes an advertisement requires little more than a headline and a visual to stop the reader and communicate the idea. But what's truly essential in effective wordplay is clarity. Being clever without being clear is a waste of words.

As you write, remember to keep it simple. Use the fewest words possible to introduce one central idea. But also keep in mind, concerning simplicity, appearances can be deceiving.

Simple words can represent complex concepts, ranging from Volkswagen's *sui generis* 'Lemon' to Altoid's amusing 'Nice Altoids'. The former is a self-deprecating reference to the Beetle. The latter substitutes the product name of a very strong breath mint for something that sounds like a human muscle.

Guidelines for wordplay:
1. Use only a few words to explain something complicated.
2. Risk a pun.
3. Say something with a double meaning.
4. Be irreverent.
5. Make fun of the name of the product.

Puns, these days, are risky business. But brilliant puns work. Anything brilliant can break any rule.

Paul Silverman, Saatchi & Saatchi advertising, Los Angeles, in *The Copywriter's Bible: How 32 of the World's Best Advertising Writers Write their Copy*, Hove, U.K.: RotoVision, 2000

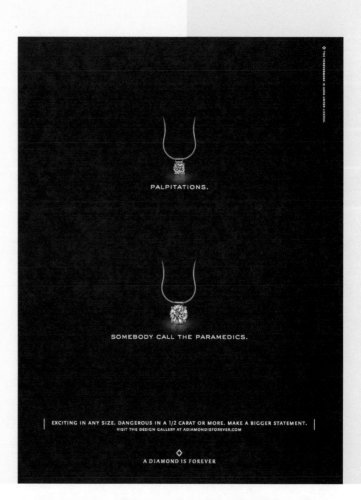

PALPITATIONS.

SOMEBODY CALL THE PARAMEDICS.

EXCITING IN ANY SIZE. DANGEROUS IN A 1/2 CARAT OR MORE. MAKE A BIGGER STATEMENT.
VISIT THE DESIGN GALLERY AT ADIAMONDISFOREVER.COM

A DIAMOND IS FOREVER

WHERE'D YOU GET THAT DIAMOND?

WHERE'D YOU GET THAT MAN?

NOTICED IN ANY SIZE. COVETED IN A 1/2 CARAT OR MORE. MAKE A BIGGER STATEMENT.
VISIT THE DESIGN GALLERY AT ADIAMONDISFOREVER.COM

A DIAMOND IS FOREVER

The Diamond Trading Company: A Diamond is Forever campaign
No one needs a diamond, so the job is to fan the desire for one. The
insight here is that the product is for display, and its appeal is visceral.
So the tone is fun and gossipy, smart and sexy. The copy is
unabashedly sensual, not because it can be, but because it should be.

Creative Directors	Chris D'Rozario, Ed Evangelista
Copywriter	Erik Izo
Agency	J. Walter Thompson
Client	The Diamond Trading Company

Don't be boring.

David Abbott, legendary British advertising executive, in *The
Copywriter's Bible: How 32 of the World's Best Advertising
Writers Write their Copy*, Hove, U.K.: RotoVision, 2000

Words give you a medium, if you will, and make your message part of the human thought process. Words are as portable as the human being who hears them.

James J. Jordan Jr., in Randall Rothenberg, *Where the Suckers Moon: An Advertising Story*, New York: Alfred A. Knopf, 1994

Mazda: How to Gauge a True Sports Sedan
Ideally copy isn't just read, it's followed. Wordplay allowed the copywriter to add layers of meaning, while directing the reader's attention to the most important part of the message. The wordplay also helps to create a tone that is both personal and accessible. When readers get the pun, they feel they belong.

Chief Creative Officer	John DeCerchio
Executive Creative Director	Michael Belitsos
Creative Director	Ken Camastro
Copywriter	Kip Klappenback
Art Director	Dennis Atkinson
Photographer	John Marion
Agency	Doner
Client	Mazda

The secret of all effective originality in advertising is not the creation of new and tricky words and pictures, but one of putting familiar words and pictures into new relationships.

Leo Burnett, *100 Leo's*, New York: McGraw-Hill, 1965, p. 72

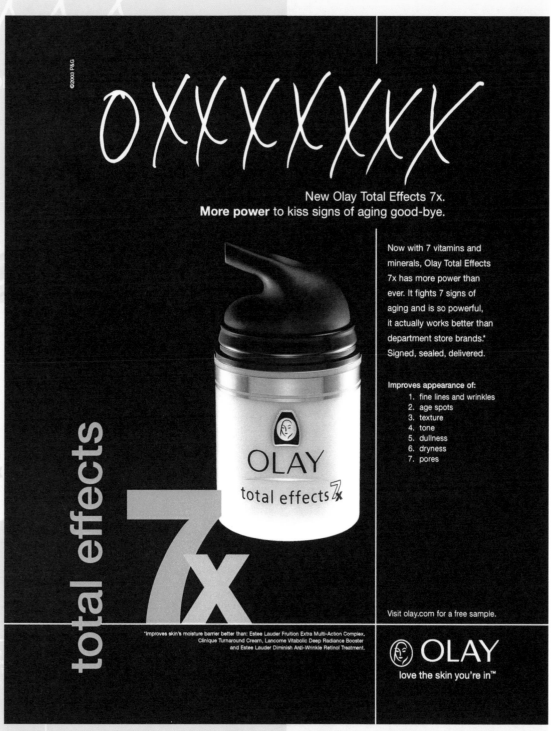

New Olay Total Effects 7x.
More power to kiss signs of aging good-bye.

Now with 7 vitamins and minerals, Olay Total Effects 7x has more power than ever. It fights 7 signs of aging and is so powerful, it actually works better than department store brands.* Signed, sealed, delivered.

Improves appearance of:
1. fine lines and wrinkles
2. age spots
3. texture
4. tone
5. dullness
6. dryness
7. pores

Visit olay.com for a free sample.

*Improves skin's moisture barrier better than: Estee Lauder Fruition Extra Multi-Action Complex, Clinique Turnaround Cream, Lancome Vitabolic Deep Radiance Booster and Estee Lauder Diminish Anti-Wrinkle Retinol Treatment.

OLAY
total effects 7x

total effects 7x

OLAY
love the skin you're in™

©2003 P&G

Pun
A humourous use of a word which suggests different meanings; frequently, words with the same sound but with different meanings. Example, 'Selling coffee has its perks.'

Double entendre
From the French meaning 'double intention'; language that can be interpreted in two different ways; often the second meaning is risqué or indelicate. Example: 'The archer took a bow before shooting his bow.'

Punchline
A phrase, statement, or sentence that makes an emphatic point; often in a joke. Example: At the hotel-lobby desk, a mother requested a separate room for her child. The reply was, 'We have a womb with a view available.'

Olay: OXXXXXXX
The use of symbols in the headline plays on the product's name by calling on the 'o' in 'Olay' as part of the letters that mean 'hugs and kisses'. The audience for this advertisement will understand the benefits laid out in the copy, including in the list. Even though various metaphors are mixed here, the takeaway message is clear: this product will make love to your skin.

Creative Director	B. Okada
Copywriter	V. Fortier
Art Director	T. Brosnan
Agency	Saatchi & Saatchi
Client	Procter & Gamble

Matter-of-fact descriptions make the improbable seem real.

Mason Cooley, *City Aphorisms*, New York: Fifth Selection, 1988

British Airways: Rest Assured

For a pleasant flight, two words equal one big promise and many general guarantees. This advertisement was written for an American audience. Its headline – clipped, precise, and ever so slightly formal – is more British English rather than American and truly in character with the brand.

Creative Director	Simon Dicketts/Matt Eastwood
Art Director	Bill Gallacher
Photographer	Richard Maxted
Agency	M&C Saatchi
Client	British Airways

Bypass the bypass.

How do you avoid bypass surgery?

Develop the first all-digital cardiovascular imaging system
that lets doctors see into your heart more clearly than ever
before. The GE Innova® 2000. It can help doctors pinpoint
coronary blockages with such precision that they may
find alternatives to bypass surgery. Now, if we could
only develop a way to get you back on that treadmill.

Visit geinnova.com for more details.

imagination at work **GE**

401(*k*)

Would you like that rolled over easy?

You've worked hard to build your nest egg. Are you sure you want to leave it behind in your former
employer's retirement plan? With the T. Rowe Price Rollover Advantage service, it's easy to take more
control of your retirement savings.

Call one of our Rollover Specialists to open your account right over the phone. They can help you
choose a T. Rowe Price fund, or you can pick from over 1,000 other funds*—all with no loads, no sales
charges, and no commissions. They can even work with your former employer to help coordinate the
rollover process. In fact, our Rollover Specialists handle just about all the IRA paperwork and will mail
you the completed forms to sign.

It's never been easier to roll over your nest egg. To open your account, call us or visit our Web site and
have your 401(k) statement in hand.

TROWEPRICE.COM/ROLLOVERADVANTAGE
1-800-250-7624

T. Rowe Price®
INVEST WITH CONFIDENCE

This service is offered by T. Rowe Price Investment Services, Inc., member NASD/SIPC. Please call to request a prospectus with more complete information, including fees, risks, and expenses; please read it carefully before investing.

GE: Bypass the Bypass
The headline is a classic pun. But, because there's nothing funny about
a heart attack, it begs the question, 'Is a pun here appropriate?'. When
you understand that this advertisement isn't intended for doctors or
heart patients, the tone makes sense. The advertisement is speaking to
people who are curious about new developments at GE and for whom
the news is good news.

Executive Creative Director	Don Schneider
Copywriter	J. Racz
Art Director	E. Van Skyhawk
Agency	BBDO New York
Client	General Electric

T. Rowe Price: Would You Like that Rolled Over Easy?
A serious subject is lightened with a bit of wordplay. The idea is two-
fold. The pun elicits a smile, and the visual suggests what could go
wrong if the investor doesn't act. The light tone, set up by the wordplay,
is maintained throughout the copy. And the copy reinforces the idea that
the process will indeed be painless.

Creative Director	Mark Kelly
Art Director	Mark Kelly
Copywriter	Belinda Broido
Agency	J. Walter Thompson

**The copy [of an ad] is merely a punning gag to distract the critical
faculties while the image goes to work on the hypnotised viewer.**

Marshall McLuhan, *Understanding Media: The Extensions of Man*, New
York: New American Library, 1964, p. 205

The 'unique selling proposition', or USP, is more difficult to conjure today.

Once a product or service succeeds, it will be copied.

The public is fickle.

The product and the idea of the product must be a single symbol.

The word 'imagery' is too often associated purely with visuals, but it is much more than that. Imagery is the conversion of an idea into a theatrical cameo, an indelible symbol, a scene that becomes popular folklore, an iconographic image; and this imagery can be expressed in words or visuals or, ideally, both.

George Lois, with Bill Pitts, *What's the Big Idea?*, New York: Doubleday Dell Publishing Group, 1991, p. 55

Do you remember the time when you didn't have to program your toaster, there were only 13 channels to choose from and you only had to deal with one kind of mail?

This chair is kind of like that.

Simple

When less really is more.

KEILHAU

Keilhauer: Simple
Chairs are like cell phones and copy machines. Manufacturers keep adding feature after feature. So this advertisement asks the potential customer, 'What do you really want from a chair?' And the name – 'Simple' – supplies all the answers. As the manufacturer has modestly declared on its website, '"Simple" spins and rolls. It goes up and down. But that's about it.' (When published in magazines, the all-words page was placed on the right side, and the image of the chair appeared on the overleaf. See also pages 29 and 62.)

Copywriter	John Pylypczak
Art Directors	John Pylypczak, Diti Katona
Photographer	Karen Levy
Agency	Concrete Design Communications Inc., Toronto
Client	Keilhauer

more than meets the eye

Rosser Reeves, who wrote both 'M&M's melt in your mouth, not in your hand', and 'Wonder Bread builds strong bodies twelve ways', also gave advertising the 'unique selling proposition' or USP. For decades, the USP informed creative work.

Today, it is not that easy. A copywriter can still invent a USP, but it might not resonate with consumers or pass governmental review. What's more, a unique thing is a rare thing, becoming rarer. Once a breakthrough product or service proves successful, it is copied and copied again. So just as the Snapple juice drinks were copied by a vast number of taste-alikes and look-alikes, likewise America's Lifetime TV network for women fostered the birth of the Oxygen channel and Jet Blue begot Song airlines.

Increasingly, customers are instinctively loyal to brands, not ideologically loyal. Relevance is what is becoming important – although the right message might have a long season.

Advertising that fosters lasting brand loyalty:
1. Seems to come from nowhere.
2. Celebrates the consumer rather than the product.
3. Continues to work very hard to distinguish the brand from its competitors.

Designed by Mark Kapka.
List price $620.
Please contact Keilhauer for your nearest representative 1 800 724 5665.
www.keilhauer.com

Do you remember the time when you didn't have to program your toaster, there were only 13 channels to choose from and you only had to deal with one kind of mail?

This chair is kind of like that.

Simple

When less really is more.

To get your ideas across, use small words, big ideas and short sentences.

John Henry Patterson, in Ted Goodman, *The Forbes Book of Business Quotations*, 1997, New York: Black Dog & Leventhal Publishers, 1997, p. 435

Heller Ehrman v. Boundaries

Perhaps a law firm need not exist inside the legal-sized parameters of tradition. Maybe it lies outside of convention. Maybe it crosses lines of formality. Maybe it recognizes a need to overstep the expected. And, quite possibly, it realizes that inspired acts of tenacity and imagination are the only way boundaries get pushed. | Heller Ehrman | ATTORNEYS | Challenging the laws of convention.™

Heller Ehrman: Heller Ehrman v. Boundaries
This advertisement reads like the closing statement of a trial – from the adversarial headline (with 'v.' for 'versus') to the measured cadence of the prose. The medium is the real message here. The act of advertising in itself is, as the tagline claims, 'Challenging the Laws of Convention'.

Copywriter	Jody Horn
Art Director	Gregg Foster
Photographer	Chris Wahlberg
Agency	Publicis USA
Client	Heller Ehrman

The PT Turbo

The new 215-horsepower PT Turbo. Houston, we have liftoff. chrysler.com

CHRYSLER
Drive = Love

x 215^{hp}

PT TURBO
t's the fun of a roller coaster with an extra blast of power.
The all-new PT Cruiser Turbo. With a performance-tuned
suspension and 215 horses, it's got the power to do anything—except maybe the loop-de-loop. For more information, call us at 1.800.CHRYSLER or visit chrysler.com

CHRYSLER
Drive = Love

Chrysler: 'PT Cruiser-Shuttle' and 'PT Cruiser-Roller Coaster'
Automobile advertising is almost always about the fantasy of driving.
This car is about fun. The experience of fun is almost all this
advertisement needs to promise. So, when introducing a new, more-
powerful version, promise even more fun.

Ex Creative Director	Bill Morden
Copywriter	Tim Thomas
Art Director	Steve Glinski
Agency Account Management Team	
Group Account Director	Katie Brown
Account Supervisor	Andrea Marcaccio
Account Executive	Jeff Sayen
Client	
Director,	
Chrysler Communications	Bonita Stewart
Senior Manager,	
Chrysler Advertising	Oliver LeCocq
Agency	BBDO Detroit
Client	Chrysler

**We grew up founding our dreams on the infinite promise
of American advertising. I still believe that one can learn
to play the piano by mail and that mud will give you a
perfect complexion.**

Zelda Fitzgerald, American writer, in Robert Andrews, *The
Columbia Dictionary of Quotations*, New York: Columbia
University Press, 1993, p. 18

Haven't heard we make the world's most powerful jet engine?

Shhhh. We're keeping it quiet.

Thanks to an ingenious, composite front fan, the innovative **GE90-115B** combines record-setting high power with remarkably low noise. You might say it's broken a new kind of sound barrier.

Visit ge.com to learn more.

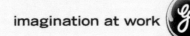

imagination at work

An image…is not simply a trademark, a design, a slogan or an easily remembered picture. It is a studiously crafted personality profile of an individual, institution, corporation, product or service.

Daniel J. Boorstin (1914-2004), American historian, in Randall Rothenberg, *Where the Suckers Moon: An Advertising Story*, New York: Alfred A. Knopf, 1994, p. 12

Nice thing about a wind farm: all year it's harvest time.

Now clean wind energy is always in season, thanks to a revolutionary **GE wind turbine** that's 40 stories tall, with blades almost as wide as the wingspans of two jumbo jets. It's a giant step in the direction of renewable energy. Isn't that a breath of fresh air?

imagination at work *GE*

GE: Haven't Heard… and Nice Thing…
This campaign launched GE's 'Imagination at Work' positioning. Notice that the slogan's three words marry the most human aspect of technology to the most practical concern of business. The tone is light, fast, and positive. This and the other advertisements in the campaign are not intended to sell products, but rather the idea that GE manufactures real products for the real world.

Executive Creative Director	Don Schneider
Copywriter	David Johnson
Art Director	John Leu
Agency	BBDO New York
Client	General Electric

In the factory we make cosmetics; in the drugstore we sell hope.

Charles Revson, founder, Revlon, in Michael Jackman, *Crown's Book of Political Quotations*, New York: Crown Publishing, 1982, p. 2

To be believed, make the truth unbelievable.

Napoleon Bonaparte (1769-1821), one of the greatest military commanders in history and Emperor of France, quote from *Oxymoronica: Paradoxical wit and wisdom from history's greatest wordsmiths*, by Dr Mardy Grothe, New York: HarperResource (an imprint of HarperCollins), 2004

Once upon a time,

there was a company with a terrible

problem: their servers just kept crashing.

So they bought Magic Server Pixie Dust. Simply

sprinkle on the Pixie Dust, and crashed servers would

suddenly come back to life. Sprinkle it on regularly, and they'd

never go down. Servers would run themselves. Repair themselves. *On demand.*

People were stoked. They could devote more attention to their other business

problems. It seemed almost too good to be true. The truth is, it didn't exist.

AND THAT'S WHEN THEY CALLED IBM.

In the *on demand* era, servers will need to have the ability to repair crashes before

they happen. To also protect themselves and manage themselves in ways never before

imagined. This is the kind of autonomic, *on demand* technology IBM is building

for the new "always on" environment. Not Magic Pixie Dust. Visit **ibm.com**/ondemand

IBM.

@business on demand

IBM: Once upon a Time...
As technology becomes more complex, there's an increasing public perception that it resembles magic. So why not tell a technology story with a fairytale? The approach may seem far-fetched, but a storybook approach makes reading about the offering a pleasure. It also suggests that, for those who buy the product, their story will also end 'happily ever after'.

Creative Directors	Jeff Curry, Tom Bagot
Copywriter	Lisa Topol
Art Director	John Lamacchia
Agency	Ogilvy & Mather New York
Client	IBM

Intel: Unwire campaign

Here, a single word is sufficient to both introduce a complex technology and to describe its benefits. It also makes a quick, hip and modern promise: this is about more than impersonal wireless technology. This is about license and empowerment. 'Unwire' is something you choose to do. It is not something done to you.

Copywriters	Steve Mulliken, Ken Segall
Art Directors	Marcus Kemp, John Rea
Agency	Euro RSCG Worldwide
Client	Intel

IBM PCs use genuine Microsoft® Windows®
www.microsoft.com/piracy/howtotell

on paths that have yet to be traveled
Dean Kamen, *Inventor, Segway Human Transporter*

ThinkPad ● Where do you do your best thinking?

IBM

Integrated dual antennae on select models for improved signal
strength.¹ Software for easier connectivity to the network when
you're on the road.² **Wireless innovation.** It's just one of the
reasons why some of the world's most successful people choose
ThinkPad® notebook computers. Select models feature a Mobile
Intel® Pentium® 4 Processor-M for outstanding performance and
mobility. Call **1.877.thinkpad** or visit **ibm.com**/thinkpad/think

IBM: On Paths... and At Table #80...
In these advertisements, the product endorsement comes from
someone who has succeeded brilliantly in his career but isn't a
household name. Readers may not recognise him at a glance, nor the
experts pictured in other advertisements in the campaign. But once the
copy introduces him, the value of the association becomes clear. In this
case, savvy, creative people will think that this product is indispensable.

Creative Director	John McNeil
Copywriter	Kristen Lewis
Art Director	Harry Bernstein
Photographer	Christopher Morris/
	VII Photos + the campaign IBM Thinkpad
Agency	Ogilvy & Mather New York
Client	IBM

endorsement. **real** and **imagined**

**Endorsements, real and imagined,
populate advertising.**

Famous faces and voices appear as
spokespeople and in cameos to sell every
conceivable product. Celebrities portray
themselves and even allow themselves to be
cast contrary to their image.

It seems that celebrities are everywhere and
that no one is too important or too rich to
say 'No'. Advertising agencies for some
companies, such as The Gap, cast huge
stars as well as somewhat known people.
Talent agents describe the latter as being
'just under the radar'. In fact, renowned
feature-film directors shoot commercials as
well as appear in them. Politicians, clergy,
athletes, artists, poets – all happily endorse
products, goods, and services.

Celebrity, in all its forms, is an aspect of the
creative content of advertising. This is why
copywriters are asked to put faces to ideas
and voices to concepts. They're also
expected to know who is big, who is on the
way up, who is falling, and who is ready for
their comeback.

Celebrity isn't a substitute for a good idea,
but it may be the next best thing.

Celebrities provide:
1. Believability.
2. Panache.
3. Respectability.
4. Noise.

No celebrity these days is
too big to sell something.

The celebrity is part and
parcel of the advertising
message.

Celebrities become the
faces of ideas and voice
of content.

Be aware of who is famous
now and who isn't anymore.

at table #80, dreaming up restaurant #5
Keith McNally, Restaurateur of Balthazar, Pastis, Pravda and Lucky Strike, New York City

ThinkPad ● Where do you do your best thinking?

IBM

**When a Big Idea celeb campaign has the power to become new language and
startling imagery enters the popular culture, advertising communication
takes on a dimension that leaves competitive products in the dust. When
celebrity ...is transformed into $ellebrity.**

George Lois, *$ellebrity: My Angling and Tangling with Famous People*, London:
Phaidon Press 2003, Introduction

"To me documentary photography is about human dignity."

Hands: Sebastião Salgado, photographer
Tool: LEICA M7

Heinz/Lenz/Zijoa

www.leica-camera.com

Leica   my point of view

Leica Camera Inc. / 156 Ludlow Ave. / Northvale, NJ 07647 / USA / Telephone 800-222-0118 / literature@leicacamerausa.com

Leica Camera: 'To Me Documentary Photography...'
A celebrated photographer is endorsing an acclaimed camera in an
advertisement that's both artful and serious. The subtle use of celebrity
here conveys important messages: this camera is about the pictures it
takes. It's a serious instrument and not merely a status symbol.

With thanks and acknowledgement to Leica.

Today, alas, without heroes, we must do with celebrities.

George Lois, 'Introduction', *$ellebrity: My Angling and Tangling with
Famous People*, London: Phaidon Press, 2003

human dignity."

The business of the advertiser is to see that we go about our business with some magic spell or tune or slogan throbbing quietly in the background of our minds.

Marshall McLuhan, 'The Age of Advertising', *Commonweal* magazine, 1953, p. 557

"Without a good eye no good photographs.
But without good hands no photo at all."

Hands: William Klein, photographer
Tool: LEICA M7

my point of view

"I capture nature in my pictures,
so that it may sustain in reality."

Hands: Norbert Rosing, photographer
Tool: LEICA R8

my point of view

About the debut of John F. Kennedy Jr.'s *George* magazine:
Celebrity distorts democracy by giving the rich, beautiful, and famous more authority than they deserve.

Maureen Dowd, American newspaper columnist, 'Giant Puppet Show', *The New York Times*, September 10, 1995

In a consumer society, the lives of the celebrities are not merely guideposts from which people can take their stylistic cues. They also embody every consumer's dream of what it would be like if money were no object.

Stuart Ewen, *All Consuming Images: The Politics of Style in Contemporary Culture*, New York: Basic Books, 1999, chapt. 5, p. 94

To me, success is a 35 minute lunch.

At a restaurant, not my desk.

Means I'm not wasting time doing the

same data management task again and

again and again and...well, you get it.

Save the day.

V2X Subsystem

Consolidate your work by consolidating data from all your different systems. One way is with a V2X Shared Virtual Array subsystem and SnapVantage software to unite all your Linux virtual servers. Or an L5500 automated tape library and T9940B tape drive. There are other ways, too. We'll help find the one that's best. So storage administration takes a smaller bite out of your day. Learn more about this story and other ways we can help you at www.savetheday.com

STORAGETEK® 'Save the Day.'™

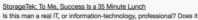

StorageTek: To Me, Success Is a 35 Minute Lunch
Is this man a real IT, or information-technology, professional? Does it matter? If the reader identifies with his story, then the story will seem true. What makes an anecdote believable is what makes it persuasive. If readers identify with the premise, they'll believe the solution, too.

Creative Director   Steffan Postaer
Copywriter   Mark Anderson
Art Director   Greg Auer
Photographer   John Offenbach
Agency   Leo Burnett USA
Client   StorageTek

They're fans.

MANDARIN ORIENTAL
THE HOTEL GROUP SM

Find out why Dame Edna & Barry Humphries are fans at www.mandarinoriental.com • BANGKOK • GENEVA • HAWAII • HONG KONG • JAKARTA
KUALA LUMPUR • LONDON • MACAU • MANILA • MIAMI • MUNICH • NEW YORK • SAN FRANCISCO • SINGAPORE • SURABAYA • TOKYO (2005) • WASHINGTON D.C.(2004)

<u>Mandarin Oriental: Fan campaign</u>
The nice twist here is casting celebrities as 'fans'. But it isn't simply
cleverness. It's a discreet way of acknowledging the hotel's ability to
satisfy its celebrated clientele. The implication is if they can turn a star
into a fan, they will make a fan of you too.

Creative Director	Alan Jarvie
Photographer	Patrick Lichfield
Agency	M&C Saatchi
Client	Mandarin Oriental Hotel Group

A celebrity is one who is known to many persons he is glad he doesn't know.

H.L. Mencken (1880–1956), American journalist, 'Sententiæ: The Mind of Men', *A Mencken Chrestomathy*, New York: Alfred K. Knopf, 1949

Alaris: Nurse/Take Good Care of Yourself

Find out what your audience experiences. Then, write about that experience. Don't embellish it, and certainly don't romanticise it. Don't be afraid to be emotional. Tell the truth, the harder the better. The key is to make the benefits real, anything less and you'll lose them.

Creative Director/Art Director	Dean Alexander, Robert Sawyer
Creative Director/Copywriter	Robert Sawyer
Design Production	Paul Rodriguez
Design Firm	Alexander Design Associates Inc.
Account Directors	Peter Nolan, Dana Weissfield, Audrey Ronis-Tobin
Brand Marketing Specialist	Trudi Bresner
Agency	T. Bresner Associates
Client	Alaris Medical

**Dean Hashimoto,
A.B., M.S., M.D., J.D., M.O.H., and now, finally, IRA.**

As a man who's devoted his life to the pursuit of knowledge, Dean Hashimoto wasn't going to pick a retirement plan

without first doing his homework. That's why he chose an IRA from us, the people with over 80 years' experience

managing portfolios for the world's sharpest minds. After discovering that our IRAs offer a variety of investment choices

and low expenses, he decided to add one to his resume. A wise choice, by a very wise man.

Log on for ideas, advice, and results. TIAA-CREF.org or call 800.842.2776

TIAA CREF

*Managing money for people
with other things to think about.*℠

RETIREMENT | INSURANCE | MUTUAL FUNDS | COLLEGE SAVINGS | TRUSTS | INVESTMENT MANAGEMENT

Dean Hashimoto became a participant in 1989. TIAA-CREF Individual and Institutional Services, Inc., and Teachers Personal Investors Services, Inc., distribute securities products. For more information, call (800) 842-2733, ext. 5509, for prospectuses. Read them carefully before investing. © 2002 Teachers Insurance and Annuity Association–College Retirement Equities Fund (TIAA-CREF), New York, NY 10017. Dean Hashimoto was compensated.

TIAA-CREF: Dean Hashimoto

This is an example of credibility being in the details. Highly educated people love to use the abbreviations of their university degrees. Thus, those in the headline introduce Dean Hashimoto as a physician and an attorney. The idea is that this very accomplished man knows what he doesn't know. So he chose this company to manage his assets, insinuating it's the smart choice for everyone.

Creative Director	Michael Ward
Copywriters	Michael Ward, Curt Mueller
Art Directors	Don Creed, Steven Grskovic
Photographer	Brad Harris
Talent	Dean Hashimoto
Agency	Ogilvy & Mather Advertising
Client	TIAA-CREF

We lose sight of the men and women who do not simply seem great because they are famous but are famous because they are great. We come closer and closer to degrading all fame into notoriety.

Daniel J. Boorstin (1914-2004), American historian, *The Image: A Guide to Pseudo-Events in America*, New York: Harper, 1961, chapt. 2

Globalism is not new to advertising.

Advertising agencies were among the first businesses to develop a global reach. Today, the money spent on advertising is increasing faster in ratio to populations and, ironically, to personal income. While most advertising remains local, business dreams have become global. Multinational companies and their primary agencies aspire to iconic campaigns that will be understood by potential consumers everywhere. To have this reach be effective, a global voice has to be developed – or a simple concept that's based on universal truths. With a nip here and a tuck there to adjust for cultural or national nuances, a global voice can be created.

Cross-fertilised ideas already exist. Creative advertising people jump from city to city, country to country. And, even if they don't physically move, their concepts and practices do.

Advertising that reaches a global audience should:
1. Feature copy that will be understood by most people.
2. Call on aspects of popular culture that has no borders.
3. Develop brand images that are universal.
4. Be sensitive to all cultures.

global voice

If you would win a man to your cause, first convince him that you are his sincere friend. Therein is a drop of honey that catches his heart, which, say what you will, is the great high-road to his reason and which, when once gained, you will find but little trouble in convincing his judgment of the justice of your cause.

Abraham Lincoln (1809-1865), American president, in an address to Washingtonian Temperance Society, Springfield, ILL., February 22, 1842

Win the heart and the mind will follow.

Roy H. Williams, *The Wizard of Ads: Turning Words into Magic and Dreamers into Millionaires*, Austin, TX.: Bard Press, 1998

Develop simple iconic advertising campaigns rather than text-driven ones.

Keep abreast of world trends.

The whole world is watching.

This is the hat that built the City.

This is the hat Otis tipped to the crowd, as he called out "All safe," after cutting the rope, that had held up the platform, that was caught by the safety, and so introduced the elevator that would build the modern cities of the world.

Over the last 150 years, the men and women at Otis—from mechanics and metallurgists to secretaries and scientists—have built the company, which built our cities. Today, we thank you for your brilliant contribution to a brilliant tradition.

OTIS

These are the glasses that built the City.

These are the glasses worn by the chief engineer, who, for 40 years, oversaw countless innovations that turned passengers' anxiety into comfort, until the act of riding an elevator required no more thought than pushing a button.

Over the last 150 years, the men and women at Otis—from mechanics and metallurgists to secretaries and scientists—have built the company, which built our cities. Today, we thank you for your brilliant contribution to a brilliant tradition.

OTIS

We invented a language owned by our client that works as well in English as it does in Cantonese, and in Mandarin as in Portuguese. By turning Motorola into 'Moto', we created a global shorthand.

Dan Burrier, creative director, Motorola account, Ogilvy & Mather, New York City, told to Robert Sawyer

These are the shoes that built the City

These are the shoes, worn by the man who, for almost 40 years, traversed the Island to help install and manage the 1,600 elevators, escalators and travolators that transformed Singapore from a provincial City into one of the Dragons of Asia.

Over the last 150 years, the men and women at Otis—from mechanics and metallurgists to secretaries and scientists—have built the company, which built our cities. Today, we thank you for your brilliant contribution to a brilliant tradition.

OTIS

Otis: Built the City campaign

Otis, the elevator company, does business in more than 200 countries. For its 150th anniversary, it wanted to create a template for a global-advertising campaign that would work in any language. The developed concept is a single format – icon and story. It's usable as is, or it can be altered to honour an individual or to celebrate something of local significance. This approach enables Otis to control its global message while remaining sensitive to cultural issues.

Creative Director/Art Director	Dean Alexander
Creative Director/Copywriter	Robert Sawyer
Agency	Alexander Design Associates
Client	Otis

MOTOROLA *intelligence everywhere*

V70

贴身 MOTO

跨世纪的创意没分寸。就如 V70 的前卫设计。全方位呈献 360 度旋转揭盖。纤巧之中 MOTOGLO 键光闪烁。要你身上的每一分每一寸。穿出个性戴出精彩。

Motorola: Moto campaign

A global voice isn't imposed; it's heard. Here, rather than force an idea on the reader, the creators of this campaign listened to one. They heard consumers call it 'Moto' – and let the usage prevail. Consumer vernacular, plus luck with phonetics, led to what the creators of this campaign call the Moto-Code. 'Moto' is simple, smart, elastic, and apparently universal. The result: copy that makes a meaningful connection between the brand, the consumer, and the advertising. The poster here, part of a campaign, works as well in English as it does in Japanese (as it does in Portuguese, see page 76).

Creative Directors	Bill Oberlander, Dan Burrier
Art Director	Michael Paterson
Copywriter	Chris Skurrat
Photographer	Platon
Producer (Art Buyer)	Leslie D'Acri
Agency	Ogilvy NY
Client	Motorola

Intel has an urgent message for the wired world:

Advertising, whether or not it sells cars or chocolate, surrounds us and enters into us, so that when we speak we may speak in or with reference to the language of advertising and when we see we may see through schemata that advertising has made salient for us... [S]trictly as symbol, the power of advertising may be considerable.

Michael Schudson, Advertising, *The Uneasy Persuasion: Its Dubious Impact on American Society*, New York: Basic Books, 1984, p. 210

Ethics still matter, regardless of how big an organisation becomes. Stupid old concepts like integrity, conscience, and character still have a role to play in this global marketplace.

Dan Wieden of Wieden + Kennedy in *one. a magazine*, The One Club for Art and Copy, vol. 6, no. 2, theme 'think small', fall 2002

Introducing Intel® Centrino™ mobile technology. The new wireless notebook technology designed specifically for the wireless world. It not only lets you work, play and connect without wires, it enables extended battery life in a new generation of high-performance notebooks that are thinner and lighter. This is your invitation to unwire your life.

centrino™ MOBILE TECHNOLOGY

Unwire.

intel.

Intel: Urgent Message (Brochure)
The desire to be modern and free is universal. 'Unwired' promises both. (*Kabel ab*, in German and *sin ataduras* in Spanish mean 'unwired'.) The practical benefit is about business, but 'unwired' can metaphorically extend into life itself. The word translates clearly yet it's also used in English in non-English-speaking markets – a new word for a New World. The text of the advertisement is stripped down, uncomplicated, and benefit-driven...so the promise of new possibilities is both credible and achievable.

Copywriters	Steve Mulliken, Ken Segall
Art Directors	Marcus Kemp, John Rea
Agency	Euro RSCG Worldwide
Client	Intel

u have to understand that there are currently only about 4 or 5 million cars in China. w, to a capitalist, to a businessman, that's an opportunity; it's a chance to create the rld's biggest car market; it's a chance to cash in on the big one.

bert Chao Gunther, president, Public Media Center, San Francisco, quoted in Jean bourne (presenter), Harold Boihem and Chris Emmanouilides (producers), *The Ad and The* , 1996, 57 min., California Newsreel

chapter **04**

hat's a sprint triathlon?

interactive
channels

It's about time

Pervasive Computing delivers mobile
solutions that accelerate business.

⊕ Learn more

Download y
Pervasive
Computing
screen sav
today (2 Mb

More demo

eas

ervasive computing
usinesses to create
and services for a new
of computing devices

mobile solutions & contact

solutions that help

Why IBM

Learn why IBM is the right choice

Freedom - IBM pervasive computing
and open standards

Innovation - Leadership in multimodal
technologies

Globalizing e-business - Learn more

Get your
Contact cer
and
Mobile
e-business
info kits tod

More literat
(whitepaper
brochures,

Websites, interactive kiosks, electronic signage, and other interactive channels demand no more or less of copywriters than other media.

Even though interactive space is both new – and continuously evolving – success here depends on good ideas expressed well. Good writing is just as necessary in this medium as any other. The difference is that it is considerably more specific. One application may require the focus and austerity of a recipe. Another may be informed by flights of fancy.

In the interactive sphere, copy should anchor ideas and concepts. Words are critical but must conform to the medium – in the way that a movie requires a script, a website needs a narrative.

What's exceptional here is the variety of writing. Your work may be a single word, 'go', to point direction, or a phrase that punctuates tone and manner. You may find yourself writing pages of descriptive information. The good news for writers is this: remove the mystique, and an interactive site is just another advertisement, like a TV spot or a brochure. It's just another business tool, another educational platform, or another source of entertainment.

Writing for the Web and writing a direct-response campaign are the same. You know whom you're writing to and what moves them. Therefore, make your writing sophisticated or naïve, whatever will work best to serve the visitor to the site. Indeed, the effectiveness and results your writing produces will be measured, and this will lead to constant updates and revisions. If you know what's needed, you can just fill in the blanks. And the requirements are the same as all other media – be lucid, simple, and engaging.

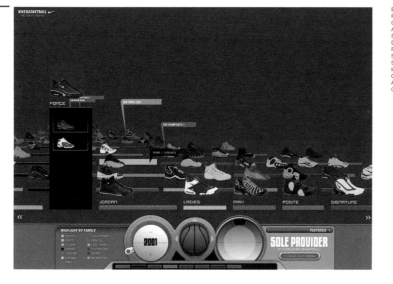

Executive Producer	Kip Voytek
Producer	Shawn Natko
Copywriter	Jason Marks
Art Director	Winston Thomas
Senior Designer	Nathan Iverson
Designer/Developer	Andrew Hsu
Flash Designers	David Morrow, Patrick Kalyanapu
Senior Engineers	John Jones, Chuck Genco, Martin Legowiecki
Senior Interaction Designer	Patrick Stern
Interaction Designer	Richard Ting
Quality Assurance Engineers	Justin Wasik, Jennifer Allen
Agency	R/GA
Client	Nike

At first the Web was like a child with incredible promise that mystified its parents. So it was allowed to run wild although it behaved less like a Mozart and more like a feral child. Today, the child is better disciplined. Business has learned what to expect from its sites and from the users who visit them. So, 'Isn't it cool' isn't the criterion any more.

Nick Law, creative director, R/GA, New York City, told to Robert Sawyer

There's a major change going on in the whole advertising community. It has to do with the fact that people are not watching 30-second commercials [on TV anymore].

Bill Squadron, 'A View of the Future: Interactive Technology Will soon Transform the Way Viewers Experience Sports on Television', *St. Petersburg (Florida) Times* newspaper, July 14, 2001

Nike Website: Basketball and Goddess

Nike is a brand powered by emotion. Its customers believe in the brand and identify with it. And the identification is unusually strong. Nike's fans demand authenticity. They want attitude. And they expect the combination of the two to be entertaining on a website. What's more, the user expects to be educated in language free of hype. So the writer or writers of the site have to know: 1. What they're writing about (shoes and apparel). 2. The context (on the street or in competition). 3. The mindset (aggression or the loneliness of the long-distance runner).

Executive Producer	Kip Voytek
Producer	Afua Brown
Associate Producer	Patrick Soria
Copywriter	Kristina Grish
Senior Designer	Rei Inamoto
Art Director	Yzabell Munson
Designer	Johanna Langford
Junior Designer	Jeannie Kang
Production Artists	Cassandra Brown, Eric Rosevear
Technical Lead	Scott Prindle
Lead Programmer	Raymond Vazquez
Flash Programmers	Chuck Genco, David Morrow, Noel Billig
Programmers	Charoonkit Thahong, Jungwhan Kim
Interaction Designer	Chloe Gottlieb
Quality Assurance	Jennifer Allen
Account Director	Karen Riley
Agency	R/GA
Client	Nike

In the interactive sphere copy isn't about words, it's about ideas and concepts.

An interactive application, like a TV spot or a sales brochure, is just another channel through which ideas are communicated.

It's widely believed that people don't like to read online, unless they are reading something they came to read.

For a writer the key is knowing what is required and then filling in the blanks.

The verbal requirements for the Web are lucidity, clarity, and simplicity.

For the writer this is the opportunity to help create 'branded' experiences.

I have a greater appreciation of copy since I've been involved in the interactive world. A successful [web] site requires a point of view …and that has to be articulated. But I suspect a new language is coming from the Web.

Robert M. Greenberg , founder, chairman, and chief creative officer, R/GA, New York City, told to Robert Sawyer

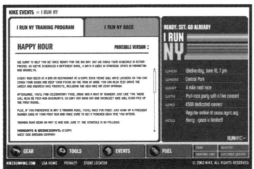

<u>Write From the Inside Out</u>
Writing well for a site like this requires more than a familiarity with the subject. The writer must write from the inside, from an enthusiast's point of view. The object isn't simply to describe, or to sell something, but to bring a story to life. If the emotions are genuine and the impression is real, then a relationship is established between like minds.

Executive Producer	Kip Voytek
Producer	Amy Weidberg
Copywriter	Joshua Bletterman
Art Director	Rei Inamoto
Senior Designer	Jerome Austria
Illustrator/Junior Designer	Mini Ham
Junior Designer	Rich Mains
Production Artists	Jeannie Kang, Cassandra Brown
Technical Lead	Scott Prindle
Senior Flash Developer	Noel Billig
Senior Flash Designers	Mathew Ranauro, David Morrow
Senior Software Programmer	Stan Wiechers
Software Engineer	Lucas Shuman, Jungwhan Kim
Interaction Director	Patrick Stern
Interaction Designer	Richard Ting, Sabine Seymour
Quality Assurance	Jennifer Allen, Justin Wasik, August Yang
Production Coordinator	Patrick Soria
Account Manager	Kate Depasquale
Agency	R/GA
Client	Nike

For marketers...the mass media are no longer the sole choice. Traditional media retain an important advantage: the 'rub-off' credibility that accrues from being part of a broadcast or publication invited into the home. But for many marketers, media advertising is a shotgun. The new technologies provide rifles, which can target prime prospects.

Stanley E. Cohen, 'The Dangers of Today's Media Revolution', *Advertising Age* magazine, September 30, 1991, p. 18

What's a banner?
It's a device (or a message in a boxed space) that will, with a couple of clicks of a mouse, take site visitors from one place and drop them off at another. Like a normal advertisement, the message in a banner should grab visitors' attention and persuade them to stop doing one thing and begin another. A banner is a unique form of advertising because it can trigger an immediate response. A coupon can lie in a drawer for weeks, a call-free telephone number can turn yellow on a bulletin board, a magazine can remain unopened for weeks. But a banner is at your readers' fingertips and, when touched, they're at the client's door immediately.

How to write for the interactive channel:
1. Understand that it's about the convergence of pictures, copy, sound, voice, music, and visual effects to create an experience.
2. Know that interactive applications don't require special writing skills but rather the ability to provide a narrative where it's needed.
3. Be open-minded and curious.
4. Appreciate that it's a collaborative medium, requiring the input of technical, business, and creative people.
5. Be authentic and sincere.
6. Know what visitors expect and give it to them.
7. Write simply in a voice that's true to the client.
8. Give the information to them fast, the way they want it.
9. Stay true to the strategy.
10. Keep the audience in front of you at all times.

The first step is always: What do we want to say…and how will we describe it? Which is why I can't envision a time when I won't be working with writers. Until we understand telepathically, there will be a need for writing.

Rei Inamoto, senior art director, R/GA, told to Robert Sawyer

IBM Website: Pervasive Computing
Motion graphics, animation, and sound may enhance a user's experience. But, concerning verbal content, good writing in this medium is simply about knowing what's required and then writing it down. The requirements here are like those of any other medium: relevance, clarity, and simplicity. It's obvious that the copy performs a number of tasks: 1. It talks about functions (menu and links). 2. It offers descriptions (text and body copy). 3. It's creative (taglines and subhead).

Executive Producer	John Antinori
Producer	Jason Tal
Associate Producer	Alan Ho
Production Coordinator	Patrick Soria
Art Director	Alex Suh
Designers	Christian Kubek, Kohsuke Yamada
Interaction Designer	Daniel Harvey
Programmers	David Yates, Jason Soncini, Sunny Nan
Quality Assurance	Juliana Koh
Account Director	Michelle Mora
Account Managers	Susanna Tully, Joy Tumbokon
Agency	R/GA
Client	IBM

chapter **05**

hat Is Altria?

brochures and other long forms

Some products and companies need more than 30 seconds or a full-page ad to convey their messages.

Complex content can be delivered in brochures and other collateral literature. These media commonly share an emphasis on content – in a format that can be pocket-sized or oversized, elaborately designed, or stripped to essentials. Advertising agencies, graphic-design firms, and in-house company marketing departments regularly produce brochures.

The difference between writing successful long-form copy and ad copy is the degree of concentration and discipline it demands. You may write an ad a dozen times before you're happy with it. That's perseverance. But long-form requires endurance. You have to be able to maintain your enthusiasm – through the thicket of detail and through the inevitable revisions as it passes through layers of client approval.

However, most advertising-industry people think that writing for collateral literature is not glamorous. Thus, many good writers avoid it. However, if you want to be a freelance copywriter or to make money writing between full-time jobs, then writing collateral material is a craft to be mastered.

Brochure and collateral-advertising writing shares some of the qualities of book and essay writing. And brochures, like books, are more permanent, less transitory than advertising in magazines and especially newspapers and on TV. They have shelf life.

The company we've grown to be.

Altria Group, Inc. is the parent company of Kraft Foods, Philip Morris International and Philip Morris USA.

A company whose past is firmly planted in success, through years of strong financial performance and global reach. Whose broad branches are blue chip operating companies that make many of the world's best-known brands: Marlboro, Maxwell House, Nabisco, Parliament, Ritz and over 160 more. Many of these brands have revenues in excess of $1 billion, and dozens more are valued at over $100 million each.

Altria is a family of companies with many roots: from a man named Philip Morris opening a tobacco shop in London; to the creation of a breakfast cereal in Battle Creek, Michigan, by C.W. Post; to a cheese company started in Chicago by James L. Kraft; to Johann Jacobs establishing a coffee business in Bremen, Germany.

Through growth and acquisition, these and other businesses have made us the broad-ranging family of companies that we are today. Our new identity will help provide greater clarity about the structure of our family of companies.

Kraft Foods Philip Morris International Philip Morris USA

Advertising is the ability to sense, interpret...to put the very heartthrobs of a business into type, paper and ink.

Leo Burnett, advertising pioneer, in Joan Kufrin, *Leo Burnett: Star Reacher*, Chicago: Leo Burnett Company, 1995, p. 54

It is insight into human nature that is the key to the communicator's skill. For, whereas the writer is concerned with what he puts into his writings, the communicator is concerned with what the reader gets out of it. He therefore becomes a student of how people read or listen.

William 'Bill' Bernbach, advertising pioneer, *Bill Bernbach Said…*, New York: DDB Needham Worldwide, 1989

What Is Altria?

Altria

Altria: What is Altria?
When a global giant changes its identity, the implications are enormously complicated. To tell the story of this magnitude, the best approach is often simplest approach. The Q&A device used here not only anticipates potentially difficult questions but also defines the terms as it frames the direction of the discussion. The result: no questions appear to have gone unanswered or become open to misinterpretation.

With thanks and acknowledgement to Altria.

Good brochure writing takes time and experience to master.

Some brochures live for years. TV and periodical advertising doesn't.

Brochure writing might not be glamorous, but it pays the rent.

The long form is a long haul.

The art of the business comes in being able to understand the problems and opportunities of any products, and then understand how to create a bond between that company or product and those people they are trying to reach.

John Stingley, in *The Copywriter's Bible: How 32 of the World's Best Advertising Writers Write their Copy*, Hove, U.K.: RotoVision, 2000

CUSTOMIZING YOUR MINI

Air Fresheners. Nothing beats that new car smell. But life happens. You suddenly take up ferret breeding. Your MINI becomes possessed by the spirit of a recently-deceased skunk. You chauffeur a couple of your alma mater's lacrosse team players who leave their sweaty gear in your backseat. Eventually, you may want to spruce things up:

Sprig of Pine. Forget the faux eau-de-public-toilette imitations. The real thing is sweeter, and it's free. Or substitute fresh rosemary from your grocer's produce section.

Peel and eat a ripe tangerine. Toss rind portion on floor area of vehicle. Park in direct sun.

Fresh-baked chocolate chip cookies. Recommended for first dates. Make them yourself, or hit the bakery on the way to her place. Don't overdo it. It's a subliminal thing. You want her thinking "nice homespun boy", not "Suzie Homemaker". (FEMALE OWNERS: Substitute fine cigars in glove box "humidor" for cookies.)

Fig. 12 MINI Magical Motoring Ball. The perfect complement to optional on-board GPS navigation. "Should I supersize my onion rings?" "Signs point to yes."

CUSTOMIZING YOUR MINI

Cockpit Toggle Switch Conversation Starters
Refer to your factory-authorized MINI owner's manual to familiarize yourself with the layout of all dashboard instrumentation. Then refer to the pre-printed labels (included with this manual) for your own personalized customization.

Proper Use of Bumper Stickers
Recommended:
1. Motorer-related stickers function like post cards to strangers from a life well-lived: "This car climbed Mt. Washington", "I got my kicks on Route 66", "Bat out of Carlsbad Cavern". (Fig. 13)
2. Law School Alumni window decals will make others think twice about messing with you in a Constitutionally-inappropriate manner. (Fig. 14)

Fig. 13

Fig. 14 What it says: You're a magna cum law-abider.

Brochure writing requires:
1. Ability to handle detail.
2. Patience with inevitable revisions.
3. Mastery of the long form.
4. Talent for telling a story.
5. Endurance.
6. Concentration.
7. Discipline.
8. Enthusiasm.
9. Practice.

Elements of a brochure are like those of a magazine layout:
1. Headlines.
2. Subheads.
3. Call-outs.
4. Sidebars.
5. Copy blocks.

Tips for writing good long-form copy:
1. Organise the story and outline or list the elements.
2. Develop a beginning, middle, and end.
3. Know all about the product or service – from objective facts to subjective truths.
4. Realise that, if readers are reading, they are serious about your product.
5. Respect them.
6. Educate them.
7. Have them feel smarter after reading the writing.
8. Provide meaningful information.
9. Use simple, clear language.

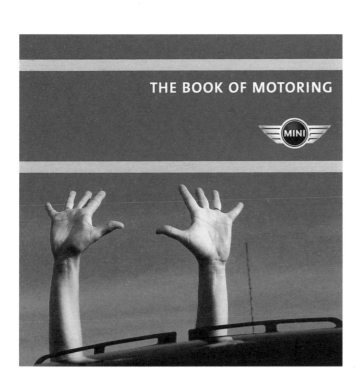

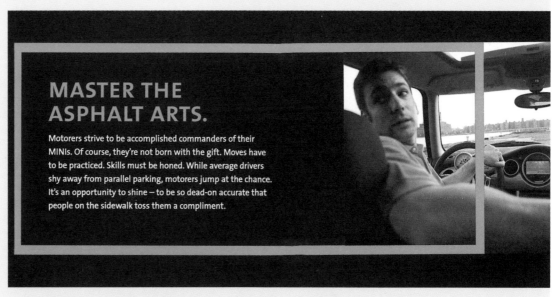

MASTER THE ASPHALT ARTS.

Motorers strive to be accomplished commanders of their MINIs. Of course, they're not born with the gift. Moves have to be practiced. Skills must be honed. While average drivers shy away from parallel parking, motorers jump at the chance. It's an opportunity to shine – to be so dead-on accurate that people on the sidewalk toss them a compliment.

Mini: The Book of Motoring/Unauthorised Owner's Manual
Educate and indoctrinate. Excite and delight. This collateral literature accomplishes what a magazine-advertising page cannot. It explores the brand in depth. A booklet can be read, re-read, referenced, shared, and kept. A brochure not only supports the regular print advertising, but also serves as an important partner in brand building. Ultimately, a brochure transcends the limited role of sales material, becoming brand-inspired literature.

Creative Director	Alex Bogusky
Associate Creative Director	Andrew Keller
Art Directors	Ryan O'Rourke, Tony Calcao
Copywriters	Steven O'Connell, Ari Merkin
Agency	Crispin Porter + Bogusky
	(Creative Dept Coordinator Veronica Padilla)
Client	Mini

■R/GA

I can write better than anybody who can write faster, and I can write faster than anybody who can write better.

A.J. Liebling, American journalist, *The Wayward Pressman* (collected writing from *The New Yorker* magazine and others), Garden City, N.Y Doubleday and Company, 1947

NIKE GODDESS

WEB SITE

www.nikegoddess.com

CHALLENGE
To build consumer awareness about the stylish and performance-driven products Nike designs for women who are active, self-confident and bold—think sexy tomboy with a sense of humor—and to create a unique e-commerce experience.

SOLUTION
Central to the site is the "Try It On" section, where users a mix and match apparel. "Try It On" is an innovative feature that makes online browsing for products fun and easy. This unique shopping experience combines ease of use and functionality with two of Nike's greatest assets, stylish products and star athletes.

TECHNOLOGY
Dynamo & Flash

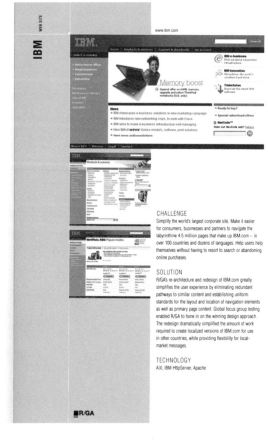

IBM

WEB SITE

www.ibm.com

CHALLENGE
Simplify the world's largest corporate site. Make it easier for consumers, businesses and partners to navigate the labyrinthine 4.5 million pages that make up IBM.com – in over 100 countries and dozens of languages. Help users help themselves without having to resort to search or abandoning online purchases.

SOLUTION
R/GA's re-architecture and redesign of IBM.com greatly simplifies the user experience by eliminating redundant pathways to similar content and establishing uniform standards for the layout and location of navigation elements as well as primary page content. Global focus group testing enabled R/GA to hone in on the winning design approach. The redesign dramatically simplified the amount of work required to create localized versions of IBM.com for use in other countries, while providing flexibility for local-market messages.

TECHNOLOGY
AIX, IBM HttpServer, Apache

■R/GA

HERE. WE MOVE WITH PURPOSE.

The landscape has shifted. Priorities have changed. Players have come and gone. Again. We've been through this before. Over the last 25 years, we've seen the industry change and change again.

We have prospered over the years by creating something unique. A studio that transcended charismatic individuals. A business that has weathered difficult times and has prospered. A company that has successfully made the transition from traditional to new media. And we have done it organically, not through acquisition, but by building from within.

What we are being asked to make today is different from what was asked last year, five years ago, 20 years ago. Our emphasis has changed from print, broadcast and feature films to interactive media, but the essence of our work hasn't changed. We continue to provide creative solutions that employ breakthrough technologies to advance our clients' objectives.

THE VIEW FROM

HERE

R/GA: Capability brochure

Tell your story in your own voice. Create content that is both unique to your client and compelling to their prospects. If there's a great deal to say, as in this brochure, then break it down into small parts with subheads and short self-contained lead-in statements. This enables readers, who might only skim through, to take away some information of substance. The technique helps serious readers to make their way from beginning to end – and feel they know the client.

Chief Creative Officer	Robert Greenberg
Copywriter	Robert Sawyer
Art Director/Designer	Nick Law
Photographer	Gary Waller
Agency/Client	R/GA

Outsourcing is not merely a viable alternative to manufacturing; in many cases, it has become the preferred means of acquiring new lines or creating custom instrumentation. KMedic, the leading supplier of orthopedic surgical instruments in the United States, is a certified vendor to many of the world's most respected orthopedic and spinal companies. In this capacity, KMedic offers companies a one-stop source for instruments when it is neither advantageous to manufacture them nor practical to acquire them piecemeal. Whether your company requires modifications of existing designs or crafting of entirely new instruments, we invite you to call and discuss how KMedic can provide the instruments you require.

KMedic

KMedic: in the Tradition of the Masters

Instrument making is a highly developed craft and the craftspeople who make KMedic surgical instruments are the modern heirs to this ancient art. It is also a vocation that has respected its traditions over the centuries. So, while new techniques have kept pace with advances in surgical practices, the essence of the craft has changed very little. Today, computers and other advanced technology aid in the manufacture of instruments, but it remains the skills of gifted instrument makers that turn raw steel into the finely honed tools ready for the surgeon's hand.

An Extension of the Hand

At KMedic we see instruments as an extension of a surgeon's hand. Therefore, we demand from our instrument makers: precision and reliability, consistency of pattern and uniform surface, all at a good value. To ensure this level of quality, every one of our suppliers must meet the requirements set by our Quality Assurance program. Only when they have met these strict standards do we qualify an instrument as KMedic Certified.

The idea that the instrument is an extension of the hand is more than a romantic notion at KMedic. It is directly related to superior performance. Surgeons who work with KMedic instruments have reported that they satisfy on many levels. First, like any well-crafted tool, they feel very good in the hands. Second, they function extremely well. Taken together, these two feelings translate into greater confidence and ease.

Evolving Tradition

As we're all aware, new surgical techniques create a continual need for improved instrumentation, as well as for the introduction of entirely new instruments. KMedic responds to these needs by working with leading orthopedic companies as well as individual surgeons to develop innovative instrument solutions. However instrumentation evolves, we firmly believe that the orthopedic community will continue to benefit from the enduring value of highly crafted instrumentation.

Helmut Kapczynski
President & CEO

What to Look for in a KMedic Certified Instrument

On the surface it's difficult to tell one instrument from another. But, in fact, many qualities distinguish KMedic Certified Instruments from those of other manufacturers. Our instruments are the product of a working knowledge of the surgeon's art, exacting manufacturing specifications and strict adherence to our Quality Assurance program. From its origins as an idea, to the crafting of the prototype, to its appearance on a surgical tray, it takes approximately 80 steps to create a KMedic Certified Instrument. At every stage of the manufacturing process, superior quality is built into our instruments. Nevertheless, before our instruments find themselves in a surgeon's hand, they are subject to an inspection process that includes:

- Visual inspection against a master sample to assure pattern consistency

- Exacting caliper and micrometer measurement of critical dimensions

- Function tests to ensure adherence to performance standards

- Surface audits to detect imperfections and irregularities

- Corrosion and hardness tests to guarantee functionality and longevity

- Maintenance of product history

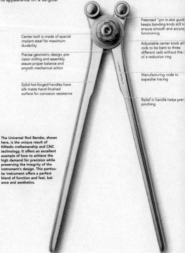

Patented "pin-in-slot guide" keeps bending knob still to ensure smooth and accurate functioning

Adjustable center knob allows rods to be bent to three different radii without the use of a reduction ring

Manufacturing code to expedite tracing

Relief in handle helps prevent pinching

Center bolt is made of special implant steel for maximum durability

Precise geometric design, precision milling and assembly assure proper balance and smooth mechanical action

Solid hot-forged handles have silk matte hand-finished surface for corrosion resistance

The Universal Rod Bender, shown here, is the unique result of KMedic craftsmanship and CNC technology. It offers an excellent example of how to achieve the high demand for precision while preserving the integrity of the instrument's design. This particular instrument offers a perfect blend of function and feel, balance and aesthetics.

Advertising is, actually, a simple phenomenon in terms of economics. It is merely a substitute for a personal sales force – an extension, if you will, of the merchant who cries aloud his wares.

Rosser Reeves, *Reality in Advertising*, New York: Alfred A. Knopf, 1986, p. 145

KMedic
Private Label

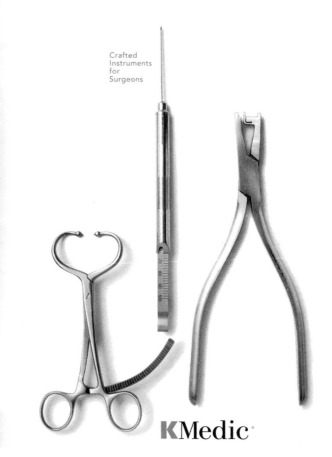

Crafted
Instruments
for
Surgeons

KMedic

KMedic: KMedic Private Label
Both professional and technical readers want to know specifics. Their
livelihoods and sense of self are built on knowledge. They think that
God really is in the details. Therefore, resist the use of generalities or
clever observations. The best way to communicate with informed
readers is to be one yourself.

Creative Director/Copywriter   Robert Sawyer
Designers/Art Directors   André Schuetz, Jea Hoon Shim
Photographer   Amos Chan
Agency   Alexander Design Associates
Client   KMedic

chapter **06**

Philip Morris Inte
Philip Morris US

names and
naming

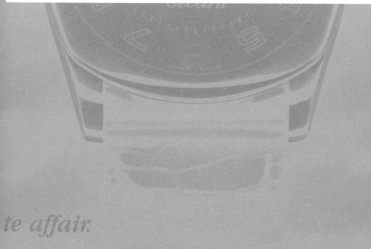

...te affair.

Naming is a business decision, not a creative one.

Everything has to be designed, and everything has to be named. New companies and products are baptised to enter and compete in the world's markets.

So who are the people who conceive the new names of companies? They can be the clients themselves, such as Arthur Anderson Consulting, which held a contest among its employees: the winning name was Accenture. Advertising agencies and branding consultants also create new names. The corporate identity firm Landor Associates helped turn Philip Morris into Altria.

If you're a writer who's been hired to develop names, you'll find yourself collaborating with philologists, semiologists, psycholinguists, other copywriters, and maybe poets. How important is the right name? Depending on various opinions, names mean less and less – or more and more. However, everyone agrees that names perform a variety of strategic functions. For example, Bell Labs became Lucent following its move to manufacturing fiber optics. 'Lucent is bigger and brighter than Bell,' Allen Adamson of Landor Associates suggests.

Names are changed when companies:
1. Merge.
2. Divest and have a new story to tell.
3. Evolve from selling products to providing services, or vice versa.
4. Turn away from the past and focus on the future.

Why some names change:

1. *Mallory Battery Company to Duracell (storage batteries):*
To shift consumers' attention from the name of the founder, whose name ceased to have meaning, to a product that could be made to mean something.

2. *Extendicare to Humana (hospital/heath-care facilities):*
To change public perception from 'warehousing' or indifferently treating people to providing a higher-level of human care and, by extension, more humane care.

3. *MMA (Micro-modeling Associates) to Plural (high-end computer systems):*
To reflect the team approach that the company adopted.

4. *KPMG Consulting to BearingPoint (business consultants):*
To suggest a new sense of purpose and commitment.

The brand gives importance to the name

In the end it's the brand that matters, not the name. James Bell, of Lippincott Mercer, believes a name may be irrelevant: 'It's what you do with it that matters. For example, nothing in "Nike" says superior athletic shoes. This is true despite the fact that it comes from the Athenian Goddess of Victory. Nike could just as well be a name for a Japanese sports sedan or a laptop computer.' The reason Nike works is because the brand has been brilliantly positioned, strenuously protected, and treated with clarity, power, and consistency.

... a rose by any other name would smell as sweet.

William Shakespeare (1564-1616), *Romeo and Juliet*, act 2, scene 2

A rose is a rose is a rose.

Gertrude Stein, 'Sacred Emily' (1913), *Geography and Plays*, Boston: Four Seas, 1922

A rose by any other name withers and dies.

Peter O'Toole as Alan Swann in Richard Benjamin (dir.), *My Favorite Year*, Warner Brothers, 1982

Naming is an inherently difficult and emotional process. It's also gruelling; in a typical presentation, 500 names are shown.

James Bell, Lippincott Mercer corporate-identity and branding consultants, New York

There are too few real words left.

Brendan Murphy, partner, Lippincott Mercer corporate identity and branding consultants, New York

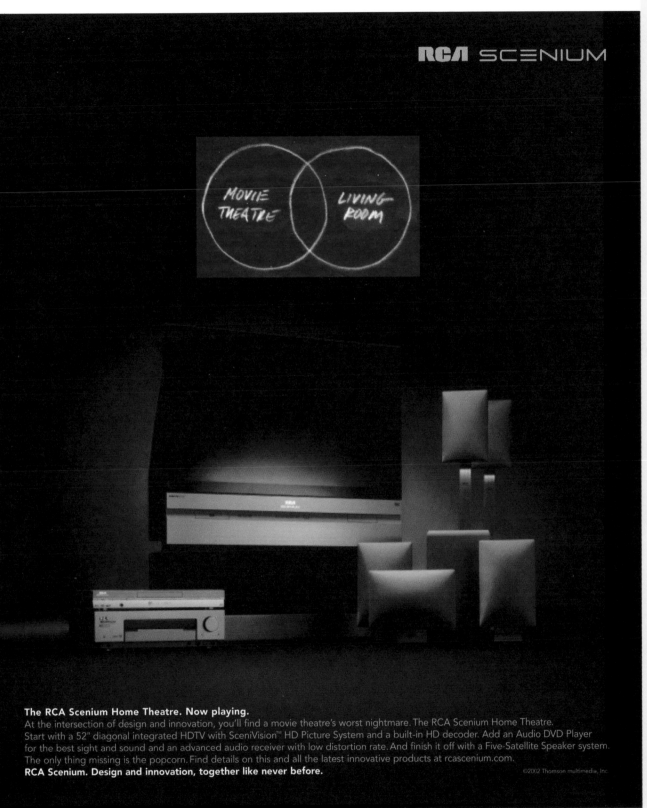

RCA SCENIUM

The RCA Scenium Home Theatre. Now playing.
At the intersection of design and innovation, you'll find a movie theatre's worst nightmare. The RCA Scenium Home Theatre.
Start with a 52" diagonal integrated HDTV with SceniVision™ HD Picture System and a built-in HD decoder. Add an Audio DVD Player
for the best sight and sound and an advanced audio receiver with low distortion rate. And finish it off with a Five-Satellite Speaker system.
The only thing missing is the popcorn. Find details on this and all the latest innovative products at rcascenium.com.
RCA Scenium. Design and innovation, together like never before.

©2002 Thomson multimedia, Inc

Metaphor
A figure of speech in which a word or phrase literally denoting one kind of object or idea is used in place of another to suggest a likeness or analogy between them. Example: 'My girlfriend is a goddess.'

Simile
A figure of speech comparing two unlike things that is often introduced by 'like' or 'as'. Example: 'Her cheeks are like roses.' Essentially identical to a metaphor, but with 'like'.

A good name is simple (JetBlue airlines for easy pronunciation and spelling).
A good name is honest (Snapple juice drinks for freshness and vigour).
A good name is relevant (Polo for an Anglo/American image and Phat Farm for urban culture).

Advertising master David Ogilvy suggested names for dozens of new products during his career; none were accepted.

Good naming requires the focus and persistence of puzzle solvers.

Problem solvers, not creative types, tend to be good namers.

RCA Scenium: Movie Theatre/Living Room
RCA chose to invent a name for a new product. 'Scene' plus 'ium' were joined to create Scenium to offer a sense theatre or, specifically here, home theatre. The goal was to create a word that suggests the convergence of media and has the feeling of 'state-of-the-art'. ('Scenium' is also used by Thomson, RCA's mother company, in Europe.)

Copywriter   Mark Ronquillo
Art Director   Niko Courtelis
Print Specialist Yajaira Fierro
Agency   Lowe
Client   Thomson/RCA

The new name Altria is intended to convey both altitude and altruism. Because we're always reaching higher and we have a commitment to social responsibility.

Louis C. Camilleri, chairman/chief executive officer, Altria, in Patricia Sellers, 'Altria's Perfect Storm', *Fortune* magazine, April 28, 2003

How a company is named:

Many marketing professionals claim that the best names are always simple and memorable. However, the sheer number of companies and the products they produce now precludes the most obvious name choices. Fortunately, any name can mean almost anything. To invent names, writers and others manipulate Latin and Greek and even Sanskrit roots, suffixes, and prefixes. Veritas is an example. Words from contemporary languages other than English are effective when they fit the product. Avaya, a telephony company, is an example.

Basic name categories:

1. Real words:
   Apple Computers, Jaguar cars, Fidelity Investments
2. Descriptive names:
   Timberline, Four Seasons Hotels, Dreamworks
3. People's names:
   Martha Stewart Everyday, Dell Computer, Veuve Clicquot, Porsche, Honda
4. Coined or invented words not in the dictionary:
   Accenture, Altria, Alaris
5. Arbitrary names, intentionally transcending or ignoring specific attributes and function:
   Motley Fool, Yahoo!, Red Hat, a route taken by various '.com' website firms
6. Historical company references:
   Wyeth, an earlier name for American Home Products; Citi, from the consolidation of Citibank's numerous financial services companies
7. Compound names, calling on recognisable words:
   Microsoft, PeopleSoft, Motorola
8. Initials and acronyms:
   BMW (Bayerischen Motor Werken), IBM (International Business Machines), ATT (American Telephone & Telegraph), BBC (British Broadcasting Company)
9. Plays on existing words:
   Xerox, Expedia, Infiniti
10. Names intended to appeal to an international audience:
    Avaya, Sony, Nokia

For more information about the Altria family of companies, visit **altria.com**.

Altria

Kraft Foods
Philip Morris International
Philip Morris USA

Altria: Altria
After 100 years, Philip Morris Companies became Altria Group. The change is largely invisible to millions of consumers who will still purchase the holding company's Kraft Foods and Philip Morris tobacco products. The change is not for the customers but for the financial community and those with an interest in how this giant manages its brands and shapes its future.

With thanks and acknowledgement to Altria.

Danaos
18kt white gold.

ROLEX
GENEVE

Cellini

A private affair.

ROLEX
Cellini

Rolex Cellini Danaos in 18kt white gold. For the name and location of an Official Rolex Cellini Jeweler near you, please call 1-800-36ROLEX. Rolex, ☵, Cellini and Danaos are trademarks.
www.rolex.com

Rolex: Cellini

How do you create an instant pedigree while calling attention to the quality and workmanship of your product? Rolex has taken the name of the celebrated Florentine sculptor, goldsmith, and writer Benvenuto Cellini, (1500–1571). The company is confident that the name will resonate with its potential customers (see also pages 79).

With thanks and acknowledgement to Rolex.

You can call something 'X' if you build and promote a smart brand around it. Put your brand in the right place, talk to the right people, with the right frequency, and any name will do.

Stacie Gray, vice-president of creative services, iN DEMAND pay-per-view TV, New York

bibliography

Bernbach W. *Bill Bernbach Said...* (1989) **DDB Needham Worldwide**

Blishen E. *Donkey Work* (1983) **Hamish Hamilton**

Bond J. and Kirshenbaum R. *Under the Radar: [Talking to Today's Cynical Consumer]* (1998) **John Wiley & Sons Inc.**

Boorstin D. J. *The Image: A Guide to Pseudo-Events in America* (1961) **Harper**

Burnett L. *100 Leo's: Wit and Wisdom from Leo Burnett* (1995) **Contemporary Books**

Cohen S. E. *The Dangers of Today's Media Revolution* in ***Advertising Age*** (1991) September 30 Issue

Designers and Art Directors Association of the UK, Designers and Art Directors Association and Dzamic L. *The Copywriter's Bible: How 32 of the World's Best Advertisers Write Their Copy* (2000) **RotoVision SA**

Donadio S. *(et al)* *The New York Public Library: Book of Twentieth-Century American Quotations* (1992) **Stonesong Press**

Ewen S. *All Consuming Images: The Politics of Style in Contemporary Culture* (1988) **Basic Books**

Fitz-Gibbon B. *Macy's, Gimbels and Me: How to Earn $90,000 A Year in Retail Advertising* (1967) **Simon & Schuster**

Fitzhenry R. (Ed). *The Harper Book of Quotations* (1993) **HarperReference**

Gallop C. in *Print* (2003) Issue LVII

Grothe M. *Oxymoronica: Paradoxical Wit and Wisdom from History's Greatest Wordsmiths* (2004) **HarperResource**

Hall P. *Tibor Kalman: Perverse Optimist* (1998) **Princeton Architectural Press**

Higgins D. *The Art of Writing Advertising: Conversations with Masters of the Craft* (1987) **Contemporary Books**

Hirshberg E. quoted in *Creativity* (2003) May Issue

Hite M. *Methods for Winning the Ad Game* (1988) **E-Heart Press**

Hitchcock G. in ***DURAK, The International Magazine of Poetry*** (1978) Issue 1

Key W. B. *Subliminal Seduction: Ad Media's Manipulation of a Not so Innocent Media* (1974) **Signet Books**

Kirkpatrick J. *A Philosophic Defense of Advertising*, **Journal of Advertising** (1986) Volume 15 Issue 2

Kufrin J. *Leo Burnett: Star Reacher* (1995) **Leo Burnett Company**

Lawner R. quoted in *Creativity* (2003) May Issue

Lears J. *Fables of Abundance: A Cultural History of Advertising in America* (1994) **Basic Books**

Lehman D. *Sign of the Times: Deconstruction and the Fall of Paul de Man* (1991) **Poseidon Press**

Leibling A. J. *The Wayward Pressman* (1947) **Doubleday and Company**

Lois G. *$ellebrity: My Angling and Tangling with Famous People* (2003) **Phaidon Press**

Lois G. and Pitts B. *What's the Big Idea: How to Win With Outrageous Ideas (That Sell!)* (1991) **Doubleday Dell Publishing Group**

McLaughlin M. *The Second Neurotic's Notebook* (1966) **Bobbs-Nerrill**

McLuhan M. *The Age of Advertising* in ***Commonweal Magazine*** (1953)

McLuhan M. and Lapham L.H. (Introduction) *Understanding Media: The Extensions of Man* (1994) **The MIT Press**

Martin K. quoted in ***One. A Magazine*** (2002) Volume 6 Issue 2

Olgilvy D. *Confessions of an Advertising Man* (1963) **Longman**

Olgilvy D. *Ogilvy on Advertising* (1985) **Vintage Books**

O' Neill G. quoted in ***Creativity*** (2003) May Issue

O' Toole J. E. *The Trouble with Advertising* (1985) **Random House USA Inc.**

Picasso P. in ***Parade*** (1965) January Issue

Poynor R. *Obey the Giant: Life in the Image World* (2001) **August; Basel: Birkhäuser**

Reeves R. *Reality in Advertising* (1986) **Alfred A. Knopf**

Rothenberg R. *Where the Suckers Moon: An Advertising Story* (1994) **Alfred A. Knopf**

Ryokan and Stevens J. (Introduction) *One Robe, One Bowl: Zen Poetry of Ryokan* (1977) **Weatherhill Publishers**

Schudson M. *Advertising, The Uneasy Persuasion: It's Dubious Impact on American Society* (1984) **Basic Books**

Sellers P. *Altria's Perfect Storm* in ***Fortune*** (2003) April 28 Issue

Starch D. *Principles of Advertising* (1985) **Taylor & Francis**

The Art Directors Club and Meyer J. M. (Ed). *Mad Ave: A Century of Award-Winning Advertising of the 20th Century* (2000) **Universe Books**

Wieden D. quoted in ***One. A Magazine*** (2002) Fall Issue, Volume 6 Issue 2 (*Think Small*)

Williams R. H. *The Wizard of Ads: Turning Words into Magic and Dreamers into Millionaires* (1998) **Bard Press**

Zimmerman J. E. *Dictionary of Classical Mythology* (1965) **Harper & Row**

index

acknowledgements

Many of the better thoughts in this book were inspired by conversations I had with a number of copywriters and creative directors who were kind enough to share their insights, thoughts and experiences. Others had in one way or another improved my own ideas. And others, still, were just instrumental in getting this book off me and on to the page. It should be understood that this is a very, very incomplete list:

Allen Adamson, Dean Alexander, Dolores Anthis, Peter Arnell, Sara Arnell, Charlotte Barnard, Kathleen Baum, Michael Beckman, James Bell, Gerd Billman, Robert Bollinger, Joe Bracken, David A. Brandt, Helen Gurly Brown, Dan Burrier, Ralph Carson, Jay Chiat, Ted Chin, Andrew Conn, James Connor, Shari Creed, Alexander Davidis, Colin Dawkins, John Dire, Ken Duskin, Stuart Elliott, David Frankfurt, Mike Frankfurt, Steve Frankfurt, Howard Goldberg, Bob Greenberg, Damien & Stacie C. Gray, Clifford Grodd, Dean Hacohen, Adrienne Hall, Gavin Harvey, Fayette Hickox, Mies Hora, Rei Inomoto, Helmut Kapczynski, Richard Kirshenbaum, William Kochi, Rick Kurnit, Rosemary Kuropat, Cedric Kushner, Catherine Larimer, Nick Law, Mike Lescarbeau, Paul Levett, Joan Levine, Jodi Lister, Jill Loewenthal, Nancy Lucci, John Luckett, Lisa Maxwell, Vander McClain, Jesse McGowen, Charles Moldenhauer, Risa Mickelberg, Brendan Murphy, Tom Murphy, Janet Odgis, Marty Orizo, Patricia Phelps, Emily Prager, Ian Reichenthal, Andrew Sacks, Andre Schuetz, Brett Sawyer, Charles Sawyer, Donald Sawyer, Ken Segall, Ken Simon, Susan Slover, Brian & Lavinia Snyder, Ron Tremba, Dieter Wiechmann, Pamela Wiedenkeller, and David Wong, Eric Chen, Frank Yeung, and the Partners of Our Place Restaurants.

With special thanks and great appreciation for their help and patience: Natalia Price-Cabrera, Editorial Director at AVA Publishing SA, Brian Morris, Publisher at AVA Publishing SA and Mel Byars, Editor and Project Manager.

Also much gratitude and affection for her tremendous endurance, I must thank my assistant, Jill Loewenthal.

And finally I dedicate *Kiss & Sell: Writing for Advertising* to my wife, Charlotte Barnard, who kept her sense of humour throughout this long process and in doing so, enabled me to keep my sanity.

Robert Sawyer